T0267280

THE MINIATURE LIBRARY OF
QUEEN MARY'S
DOLLS' HOUSE

THE MINIATURE LIBRARY OF QUEEN MARY'S DOLLS' HOUSE

Elizabeth Clark Ashby

with contributions from
Kate Heard, Kathryn Jones,
Sophie Kelly and Emma Stuart

ROYAL COLLECTION TRUST

CONTENTS

· · · · · · · · · ·

CLARENCE HOUSE

I am delighted to introduce *The Miniature Library of Queen Mary's Dolls' House*, written to celebrate the centenary of the largest dolls' house in the world.

As visitors from across the globe have found since 1924, this perfect miniature home is many things. Initially intended as a gift to Queen Mary in the aftermath of the First World War, it is also a showcase of the excellence of British and Irish craft; and a trove of unexpected, thought-provoking and witty gems: a pot of real cold cream, a Fabergé mouse, a working trouser press, a fully plumbed bathroom … Above all, perhaps, it is an unrivalled snapshot of 1920s' culture, with a library containing hundreds of printed books and drawings, and original manuscripts penned by the most significant writers of the day.

A new Sherlock Holmes tale and a famous poem about Christopher Robin nestle on the shelves with tiny volumes handwritten by novelists, including J.M. Barrie, Rudyard Kipling, Vita Sackville-West and Thomas Hardy. As E.V. Lucas wrote in *The Book of The Queen's Dolls' House*, 'How many London residences, even in Berkeley Square and Park Lane, have a library consisting of two hundred books written in their authors' own hands? I doubt even if you could find the counterpart of these in the real Buckingham Palace'.

This charming book reveals the treasures and the magic of this most unique of libraries. I very much hope that you will all enjoy it!

'A VERY GREAT TREASURE'

The Creation of a Miniature World

· · · · · · · · · · ·

An ancient philosopher writing in Greek
– And others have held the opinion before –
Declared as a fact of which few people speak,
That a very great book is a very great bore.
But let poets whose pens are invited to write
On a leaf such as this, but whose fancies are sterile,
Take courage, for here, by one fact of their plight,
They are safely secured from one species of peril.
For if length be an evil, they can't be too long,
The page puts a stoppage to metre and measure;
Let us hope 'twill be found when they cease
    from their song,
That a very small book is a very great treasure.

W.H. Mallock, 'ΜΕΓΑ ΒΙΒΛΙΟΝ ΜΕΓΑ ΚΑΚΟΝ' ['Great book, great evil'], from his Dolls' House Library book, *Verses*

'A VERY SMALL BOOK IS A very great treasure', wrote the poet W.H. Mallock in the miniature volume he contributed to the Library of Queen Mary's Dolls' House at Windsor Castle. Along with many of the most popular and significant writers of the 1920s, he handwrote a dolls' book, no higher than 4 cm, as part of a scheme to create a unique miniature library that reflected the literary landscape of the time. These handwritten books (or manuscripts), together with the smallest printed books, miniaturised music scores and hundreds of postage-stamp-sized works

· ·

Opposite: Queen Mary's Dolls' House Library

by the nation's foremost artists, are a treasure trove of early twentieth-century culture.

The books are stored in a miniature room specifically built for them, where they offer tantalising glimpses of colourful and gilded spines to visitors to the Dolls' House, their covers closed and their contents unseen. Small and fragile, the books are exceptionally hard to display open in an exhibition or reproduce faithfully, yet here, through digital manipulation of select pages photographed while the books were barely open, we are able to open up Queen Mary's Dolls' House Library, allowing readers to browse its shelves and view the pages of its tiny books. Through close examination of the books and artworks, and through documentation and correspondence kept in the Royal Archives, the whole story of Queen Mary's Dolls' House Library is told here for the first time.

'DOLLYLUYAH!'
The Dolls' House

Queen Mary's Dolls' House and its contents were created between 1921 and 1924 as a gift to Queen Mary (1867–1953), wife of King George V (1865–1936). The Queen was a great art collector and had a particular fondness for miniature objects. In 1921 her childhood friend and first cousin by marriage, Princess Marie Louise (1872–1956), observed her furnishing a dolls' house to sell to raise funds for the London Hospital. The Princess decided to create for the Queen a dolls' house of her own. The gift would celebrate Queen Mary's love of small things, recognise her tireless philanthropy, and show appreciation for the support she gave to the nation during

Miniature photographs of King George V and Queen Mary

Royal Souvenir, c.1900–10, enamel photograph album with gelatin silver prints

RCIN 2937835

Madam, in these bad days, when, like a barque
That has outridden bitter storms, the state
Swings in a troubled afterflood of hate
And violence; when through the night, no spark
Of windy starlight flickers down to mark
The shaken course we steer, nor to abate
The black turmoil through which, predestinate,
We fly before the wind into the dark:
When statesmen all turn tricksters; when the press
Flatters and fawns and slips base passions free;
When duty is a legend, and success
Falls at the feet of mad profusion; we,
Who love our English name, have need to bless
The Throne's devotion and simplicity.

Francis Brett Young, 'Sonnet to H.M. Queen Mary, 1922',
from his Dolls' House Library book, *Extracts from the
Work in Prose and Verse of Francis Brett Young*

W&D Downey (active 1855–1941)
*Queen Mary of Great Britain and
Ireland*, 1929, platinum print
RCIN 2912659

the First World War of 1914–18 and the
period of economic turmoil that ensued. The
House was to be funded by donation and
sponsorship, and, at Queen Mary's insistence,
profits from exhibiting it would be shared
amongst the charities of which she was patron.

Queen Mary was delighted with
her Dolls' House, and before it went on
exhibition she spent time arranging and
adding to the rooms. For the Library she
provided miniature objects to decorate
it, and offered books such as the *Royal
Souvenir*, a red enamelled photograph album
containing six tiny royal portraits.

Many of the contributors of manuscripts
to the Dolls' House Library were drawn
to the project through its association with
the Queen. For some, such as the novelists
William John Locke, Anthony Hope and
Beatrice Harraden, a major reason for writing

for the miniature library was the opportunity it gave them to express their sense of homage and loyalty to Queen Mary, as they told Princess Marie Louise when corresponding with her. For others, the Queen provided inspiration. The novelist and poet Francis Brett Young wrote a miniature book of verse and prose for the Dolls' House, including a sonnet to Queen Mary that reflected the views of those who felt she provided welcome stability.

Princess Marie Louise, the organiser of the Dolls' House project, was a granddaughter of Queen Victoria and a cousin of King George V. After her marriage to Prince Aribert of Anhalt in Germany was suddenly annulled by her father-in-law in 1900, she returned to England, where she had spent much of her childhood, and devoted herself to charitable causes, a course of action which was, as she recalled in the memoirs she published in 1956, 'the only way to prevent self-pity'.

As well as having the idea of creating Queen Mary's Dolls' House, Princess Marie Louise was heavily involved in its organisation. She was particularly busy with the creation of the miniature library, planning whom to ask to submit books and artworks, inviting contributions, chasing late entries, offering advice and encouragement, organising bookbinding and thanking participants for their efforts.

In addition to this, the Princess provided support for the artists and writers who contributed to the Dolls' House and its Library through hosting regular dinner parties to which

....

Lafayette Ltd

Princess Marie Louise of Schleswig-Holstein, 1921, bromide print

National Portrait Gallery, London

NPG AX29349

The Dolls' House being packed up to leave Lutyens' home in Mansfield Street, London, *c.*1924

Hulton Archive, Getty Images

they were invited. A patron of the arts, she already had a significant network of artist, musician and writer acquaintances, but the Dolls' House project, she recorded in her memoirs, brought her close friendship with 'many wonderful and delightful people'.

One of Princess Marie Louise's close friendships was with the renowned architect Sir Edwin Lutyens (1869–1944), whom she asked to design the Dolls' House. Increasing familiarity in Lutyens' letters to the Princess, sent over the course of the project, shows how their friendship grew.

In 1921, when work on the Dolls' House began, Lutyens had been working on a somewhat larger project – designing New Delhi in India – for nine years. Although he could be insensitive, childlike and difficult to work with, he was also humorous and sociable, and his delight in the whimsical and his large cultural network made him the ideal choice for Queen Mary's Dolls' House. He entered into the task wholeheartedly and with customary playfulness, referring to the scheme as 'Dollyluyah!'.

As well as designing the House, Lutyens, precise and controlling in the minutiae of his architectural projects, oversaw every aspect of its fitting, furnishing and decoration. He was instrumental in encouraging contributions to the project, particularly of books. He ensured the correct scale of one inch to a foot (2.5 cm to 30.5 cm) was maintained throughout, and approved or rejected miniature additions, whether they were donated or created especially. Under his supervision, the foremost craftspeople, the leading companies, and some of the most significant artists and designers of the 1920s built, decorated and provided the contents of the Dolls' House.

Construction began at Lutyens' offices in Apple Tree Yard, London, where the Dolls' House grew to 2.6 m by 1.5 m: so large that a wall at Apple Tree Yard had to be pulled down when it was moved across town to Lutyens' own drawing room, where its contents, including the library books, were assembled. On completion in 1924 the House was displayed at the British Empire Exhibition in Wembley, where it became the main attraction. After being exhibited again at the Ideal Home Exhibition in Olympia, West Kensington, in July 1925, it arrived at its final location at Windsor Castle, where it remains, housed in a room specially designed by Lutyens.

The Dolls' House has numerous bedrooms and bathrooms, several reception rooms and a substantial kitchen, along with nurseries, servants' rooms, extensive stores, garages and a landscaped garden. The Library makes it complete. To the right of the main entrance, it stretches the full depth of the House.

Equipped with modern conveniences, the Dolls' House is fully functioning. It was designed to have running water, electric lights and a working lift. The doors really lock and the Kitchen and Cellars contain real food and drink. Naturally the books needed to be real too, and they needed to be readable: while

....

The Dolls' House exhibit at the British Empire Exhibition, Wembley. From left to right stand Sir Edwin Lutyens, Queen Mary, King George V, the Duchess of York (later Queen Elizabeth) and the Duke of York (later King George VI), with others, 1924, gelatin silver print

RCIN 2303636.f

The Dolls' House in its current location at Windsor Castle

most of them are perhaps a little big to be comfortable for any dolls of the House's scale to hold, they are just about large enough for humans to read without a magnifying glass.

The Dolls' House was intended to be an ideal home, fit for royal dolls, but it also had other, more serious, purposes. It highlighted the best of British and Irish art, craft and manufacturing, in an attempt to reinvigorate bleak employment prospects: those working in the arts found that their opportunities had dwindled following the First World War.

It was also supposed to be a record of life in the 1920s for future historians. Yet, built as an ideal home for royalty with a jewel vault and a dining table that can serve 18, it was capturing a particularly privileged way of life. The realities of poverty and political crises and the social changes wrought since the end of the Victorian and Edwardian eras are hidden. Instead, the House reflects the glory days of great households. The manuscripts and artworks in the Library are an exception, in that they cover wider aspects of society and culture. Their creators have engaged more successfully with the contemporary political

and social landscape, and have better fulfilled the aim of recording life in the 1920s.

The World War of 1914–18, as well as the Russian Revolution of 1917, were shocks still resounding in 1921 when the Dolls' House was begun and the Library was being assembled. After the trauma, people needed to commemorate the dead and process their experiences. Conversely, they also needed to forget, if only temporarily. For the organisers and contributors the House provided a means of escape into an ideal, controllable world. For some it was even a home for make-believe, sentient dolls and real, magical fairies. The books and art in the Library reflect this desire both to remember and to escape.

THE ROOM

· · · · · · · · · · ·

KATHRYN JONES

THE DOLLS' HOUSE LIBRARY WAS INITIALLY thought of as the King's Library, giving the doll king sitting-room space as a counterpart to the queen's own space, the Saloon. As well as housing the books, it was intended to incorporate comfort with space for working.

Sir Edwin Lutyens' design for the Dolls' House Library resembled a number of the full-sized schemes he had worked on. The closest parallel is perhaps the library at Howth Castle in County Dublin, created by the architect in 1911, with its coffered ceiling, walls entirely lined in densely packed bookshelves, and panelled oak doors. In order to add support to the floor above the Dolls' House Library, Lutyens provided screens of walnut Ionic columns which divide the room. In the centre is an elegant neo-classical white marble and lapis lazuli chimneypiece,

the panelled oak upper part framing a portrait of Elizabeth I by William Nicholson. The hardstones used to create the fireplace were a gift from India, in acknowledgement of Lutyens' concurrent work on the new government buildings in New Delhi.

Lutyens' sketches for the room include designs for the wooden panelling and the arched niches that flank the fireplace, and house a door leading to the Upper Hall at one side, and a glass-fronted gun cabinet and safe at the other. The sketches suggest that the ceiling would be painted. The artist chosen for

....

Opposite: Sir Edwin Lutyens (1869–1944)

Plan for the Dolls' House showing the King's Bedroom and Library, 1921, pencil and coloured pencil

RCIN 934013

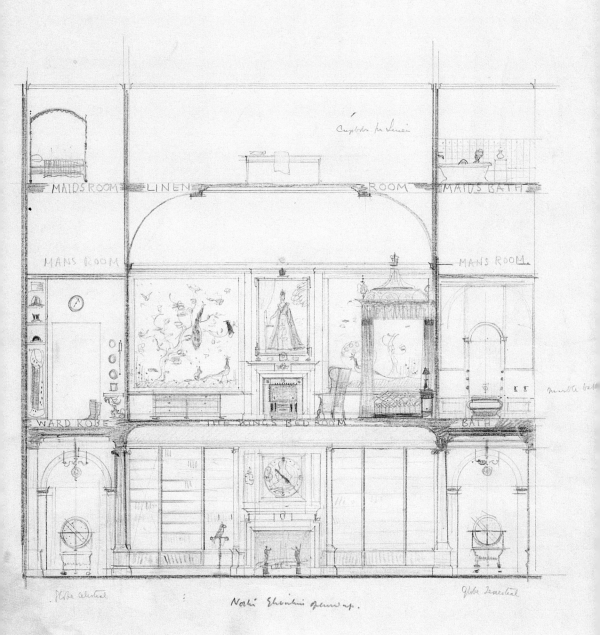

MAIDS ROOM   LINEN   ROOM   MAIDS BATH

Cupboards for Linen

MANS ROOM   MANS ROOM

marble bath

WARDROBE   THE KINGS BEDROOM   BATH

Globe Celestial   North Elevation opened up.   Globe Terrestial

this space was William Walcot, an architectural illustrator and frequent collaborator with Lutyens. Walcot's ceiling is entitled 'Hints of Roman Things' and shows classically draped figures and carved stone features.

As the working space for the doll king, the Library was furnished with a large partners' desk by the firm of Turner, Lord & Co., complete with leather top. Here he might consult the numerous despatch boxes created by one of the firms who acted as bookbinders for the Dolls' House scheme, Sangorski & Sutcliffe. The boxes were exact replicas of the versions used in the Royal Household, and they contain miniature despatches bound in silk thread from all government departments. King George V was amused by the despatch

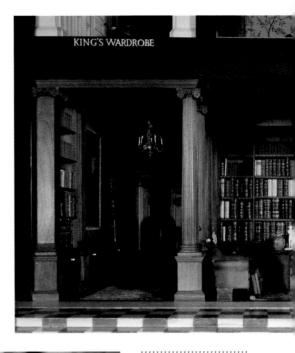

KING'S WARDROBE

Above: Queen Mary's Dolls' House Library

Left: Sangorski & Sutcliffe

*Miniature despatch box with scroll, c.*1921–4

RCIN 230696

KING'S BEDROOM   KING'S BATHROOM

boxes, and Princess Marie Louise recalls in her autobiography that he wondered how she had managed to have them copied. 'Who gave you permission?', he asked. She replied, 'no one'. There are also desk calendars, a tiny ivory paperknife incised with the royal cypher, and a magnifying glass to read the small print. A diminutive ink pen was supplied by Mabie Todd & Co. and bottles of ink by Henry Stephens. Bundles of writing paper, imitating the full-scale versions used by the King, were also provided, with matching envelopes for the royal correspondence.

The designs for the Library indicate that this was conceived as a space where the doll king might also enjoy his leisure. Luxury and comfort are provided by silk velvet rugs from the Gainsborough Silk Weaving Company, and silver chandeliers by the goldsmithing firm of Crichton Brothers. Lutyens' initial sketches include a drinks cabinet complete with miniature soda siphon and a tiger-skin hearth-rug. While not all of his ideas made their way into the House, many did, particularly the leather-upholstered seating, including two so-called 'Napoleon' chairs.

These asymmetrical chairs were based on one that Lutyens had seen in a painting of the French emperor and were a favourite of the architect himself. A small note on the sketch records 'the most comfortable in the world, recommended'. Lutyens apparently enjoyed lounging in such a chair smoking his pipe. In the Dolls' House Library too, the king was provided with both a pipe with tobacco and cigars, together with a set of matches.

Other objects associated with leisure activities include sets of playing cards, dice and a shaker, and a rosewood-and-ivory chess board and pieces by the firm of John Jaques & Son, specialists in toys and games. Royal sporting life was demonstrated by a stuffed sea trout, no doubt supposedly caught by the diminutive doll monarch himself, and by a pair of Purdey shotguns, which break and load. The guns were originally intended to be housed in the glass gun case at the back of the room, but King George V himself insisted that they be placed more prominently in the space so that the workmanship could be appreciated, and they have traditionally been shown on top of one of the folio cabinets. The King's naval background was commemorated in the House: the Library holds two small-scale globes, both terrestrial and astronomical, for navigation, and a model ship – the *Royal George* of 1788.

Sir Edwin Lutyens in a 'Napoleon' chair
Lutyens Trust Photo Archive

Queen Mary's hand may be seen at work in the Library. As the Queen became increasingly involved in the furnishing and arrangement of the interiors of the House, she provided several miniature items from her own collections. Among these were the tiny carved scarabs, originally intended to be beads, their bodies pierced for stringing, which now sit on a ledge in the Library. She was also responsible for a number of other works of art in the Library collected from around the world – a carved group of three Egyptian deities, for example, and the Asian porcelain vases. As it was Queen Mary's intention that the Dolls' House should fulfil a charitable purpose, the baize-covered card table in the room was provided by the League of Remembrance, a charity which gave work to First World War widows.

The two folio cabinets to hold the King's Library's miniature watercolour collections were supplied by the firm of Turner, Lord & Co. Although these cabinets were not ultimately used to hold the paintings, they show the same level of detail lavished on every piece in the House – the walnut veneer of the drop-front drawers is carefully cross-banded and the leather top shows gilt tooling and King George V's own cypher.

The Library's intellectual purpose is underlined by miniature bronze busts of the German writers Schiller and Goethe, and an ivory bust of Henri IV of France carved by Princess Helena, the aunt of King George V and Princess Marie Louise's mother. As well as William Nicholson's painting of Elizabeth I, two further portraits of the King's royal ancestors were hung in the space – Henry VII by Frank Reynolds, and Henry VIII by Arthur Stockdale Cope. All three were famed for their learning. The furnishing of the Dolls' House Library shows that the room was intended, above all, to function as a comfortable working library.

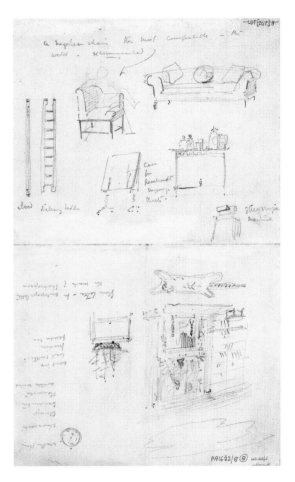

Sir Edwin Lutyens (1869–1944)

Queen Mary's Dolls' House: sketched designs for furniture and furnishings, *c*.1920–22, pencil

Royal Institute of British Architects, London

RIBA 29644

'EVERY AUTHOR OF NOTE'

··········

THE DOLLS' HOUSE LIBRARY IS THE only royal library to have been created as a discrete whole, with books commissioned for the purpose. It is formed of 595 miniature books. Of these, 176 are manuscripts: handwritten contributions from many of the most significant literary figures of the day. They are shelved alongside 132 tiny printed books, newspapers and magazines, including Bibles, railway timetables and the complete works of Shakespeare. Some of these printed items were created before the Dolls' House project, some were made specially for it and some were added afterwards. There are also 24 minuscule printed music scores from contemporary composers, and two stamp

··

A selection of books from the Dolls' House Library (from top to bottom):

Frederick Fetherstonhaugh
(1858–1931)
The Sandringham Stud Book, 1924
RCIN 1171508

W. Somerset Maugham
(1874–1965)
The Princess & the Nightingale, 1922
RCIN 1171526

Sir Arthur Wing Pinero
(1855–1934)
Little Fables, 1922
RCIN 1171539

Sir Arthur Conan Doyle (1859–1930)
How Watson Learned the Trick, 1922
RCIN 1171476

Charles F.A. Voysey (1857–1941)
Ideas in Things, 1923
RCIN 1171445

Rudyard Kipling (1865–1936)
Verses, 1922
RCIN 1171484

albums, with stamps specially miniaturised to fit the Dolls' House scale. Other miscellaneous miniature books such as blotters and visitors' books add to the collection, along with 241 blank books bound in red or blue card, created to fill up the shelves.

Works of art on paper, traditionally part of a library's holdings, are represented by three photograph albums and a staggering 774 miniature drawings, watercolours and prints, which were contributed by a broad range of British and Irish artists. These were created for diminutive portfolios kept in specially made cabinets.

While most of the miniature books in the Dolls' House are to be found in the Library, magazines can be spotted in servants' rooms, the Princess Royal has a New Testament in her room, and an 1837 almanac lies in the Queen's Bedroom. There are books of children's music in the Nursery, a scaled-down copy of *The Times* in the King's Bedroom, and a visitors' book resting on a side table in the Entrance Hall.

....

Opposite: Detail of the Library with a selection of miniature manuscripts arranged on one of the folio cabinets

The majority of the manuscript books were contributed to the Dolls' House Library between 1921 and 1923, and most of the printed books were added at the same time. These were all listed in a catalogue compiled by Library organiser E. V. Lucas (1868–1938) called *The Book of the Queen's Dolls' House Library*, published in 1924, which also reproduced much of the contents of the manuscripts.

A few books, newspapers and magazines have been added to the Dolls' House collection over the century since it was formed, and comparisons with early catalogues show that a small number have left the collection.

⸻◆⸻

The miniature manuscripts sent to the Dolls' House Library provide a fascinating snapshot of literature of the 1920s. While many of the writers copied extracts from works already published or in the process of being so, much of what was written in the little books was composed specially for the Dolls' House. Although many of these unique contributions were subsequently reproduced in the 1924 catalogue edited by E. V. Lucas, few were published elsewhere, and they remain largely unknown.

Several literary movements coincided in the 1920s as the Victorian and Edwardian eras faded but still had influence, and as the twentieth century began to bring change. Writers now described as belonging to Romanticism or Modernism, *fin-de-siècle* or First World War writing are all combined in the Dolls' House Library. Many of the time's leading playwrights, essayists, academics, journalists, poets and novelists are represented, as well as some writers who were extremely popular but are now almost forgotten.

Collections from poets include those made specially by Walter de la Mare, A.E. Housman and Rudyard Kipling. Extracts from novels were submitted by popular authors such as Elizabeth von Arnim, May Sinclair and Mary Cholmondeley, and essays were contributed by John Buchan, E.M. Delafield and former Prime Minister H.H. Asquith. Still-loved writers Siegfried Sassoon, Joseph Conrad, M.R. James, Sir Arthur Conan Doyle, G.K. Chesterton, A.A. Milne and Sir J.M. Barrie are all on the shelves.

Contributors of manuscripts were from a broad age range. A few younger writers were involved: the war poets Edmund Blunden and Robert Graves were in their twenties, as was the poet and novelist Aldous Huxley. The oldest contributor, Frederic Harrison, was in his nineties, and many of those invited, including the Poet Laureate Robert Bridges and the revered Thomas Hardy, can

be thought of as elderly, late-Victorian greats. Death was not necessarily a barrier: Robert Louis Stevenson, who had died in 1894, was felt to be of too much significance within this generation of writers to be excluded, so his friend Sir Sidney Colvin was asked to make a selection from his works.

This breadth was deliberate: writers were chosen with the intention that they be representative of British and Irish literature. A draft by E.V. Lucas of the letter that was sent to invite participation, kept in the Royal Archives, shows that his and Princess Marie Louise's aim was to have 'every author of note' represented.

The subjects covered by the books also range widely. While some of the contributions were chosen by writers as being characteristic of their output, there are, appropriately for a dolls' house, fairy tales and children's stories, from W. Somerset Maugham and Fougasse, along with accounts, maxims and poems about and from the point of view of fairies, dolls and toys. There are books written for dolls on acting, philosophy and history; and books for the use of the dolls living and working in the Dolls' House, including a cookery book, a wine cellar list and a catalogue of the art. Stories about Queen Mary's Dolls' House itself were contributed by Max Beerbohm and Vita Sackville-West, and other extraordinary houses, real and imaginary, inspired Edmund

Gosse, Sir Reginald Blomfield and E. Phillips Oppenheim. There is even a satire of the Dolls' House: a fictional account by Ronald Arbuthnott Knox, a Roman Catholic priest described at the time as 'the wittiest young man in England'. In this, a committee is tasked with a project to create a huge model of a businessman's study, ten times life size. With the character of Sanderson, an artist designing the scheme, Knox poked fun at Sir Edwin Lutyens' determination for everything in the Dolls' House to be exactly to scale.

Other topics covered include the Brontës, Christmas, gardens and the sea.

A few of the books make unpleasant reading today, due to content that is now regarded as racist and antisemitic. Overshadowing all the contributions to the Library is the First World War, which had ended only three years before books were first submitted.

The manuscripts were beautifully bound in delicate leather with gold tooling by four of the leading bookbinding firms of the 1920s: Riviere & Son, Zaehnsdorf, Birdsall & Son and Sangorski & Sutcliffe. The binderies took this opportunity to show off the skills of their artisans, and provided much of

Sanderson informed us that according to his design all the books were to be ten times as big, in each measurement, as the ordinary. Sir Ernest pointed out that at this rate each volume would be about seven feet high, almost five feet broad, and more than two feet thick. A book of such a size, he suggested, could not easily be consulted by anybody who was not endowed with the physique of a railway porter . . . . Sanderson had, it must be confessed, prepared his plans down to the last detail . . . The binding, he said, would need to be exceptionally strong . . . . (Lord Billericay, who had only just been pardoned his last offence, here disgraced himself again by proposing hippopotamus hide.)

Ronald Arbuthnott Knox, from his Dolls' House Library book,
More Memories of the Future

EX LIBRIS

their work for free. Many of the books appear jewel-like, their bindings reflecting the treasure of their contents.

E.H. Shepard, an artist working for *Punch* magazine who would later illustrate A.A. Milne's *Winnie-the-Pooh* stories, designed the bookplate that was pasted inside the front cover of the miniature books when they were bound. These tiny prints, which show a silhouette of Windsor Castle's Round Tower, measure just 1.7cm square. They can be found in nearly all of the Dolls' House Library books, excepting a handful of the printed books which are either too small or were added after 1924.

Above: E.H. Shepard (1879–1976)

Design for Queen Mary Dolls' House bookplate, c.1922, ink

RCIN 1047663.c

A simplified version of this design was miniaturised for pasting into the books

Right: E.H. Shepard's bookplate inside Fougasse (1887–1965)

J. Smith, 1922

RCIN 1171321

WOMEN

The Dolls' House Library includes works by some of the most remarkable women of the late nineteenth and early twentieth centuries. Several were prominent in the suffrage movement: when the Dolls' House was being constructed, some women – those over 30 who also met certain qualifications regarding ownership of property – had the vote (recently given them in 1918), but many were still disenfranchised until 1928.

Elizabeth Robins, an actor and writer who was the first president of the Women Writers' Suffrage League, sent in extracts from her 1908 novel *Come and Find Me*, while the suffragist Beatrice Harraden, whose contribution is taken from her first novel *Ships that Pass in the Night* (the origin of that phrase), had refused to pay income tax in 1910 after women were denied the vote in Parliament. The composer and writer Dame Ethel Smyth, a close friend of the suffragette leader Emmeline Pankhurst, was jailed for smashing a window when a member of the Women's Social and Political Union. She contributed a scaled-down music score as well as an extract from her 1921 publication *Streaks of Life*, a

Herbert Lambert (1881–1936)
Dame Ethel Mary Smyth, c.1922, photogravure
National Portrait Gallery, London
NPG AX7742

collection of autobiographical essays. The extract is about the former Empress Eugénie of France, a friend Smyth shared with Princess Marie Louise. Her choice was appropriate: the Empress collected miniature books.

Mothers and daughters are to be found in the Dolls' House. Effie Maria Albanesi, who often published under her first married name, Effie Adelaide Rowlands, contributed an extract from *The Glad Heart*, one of her numerous novels, while her daughter, the successful young actress Meggie Albanesi, signed a book collecting the autographs of those who worked in theatre. Lucy Clifford, a famed writer who usually published under the name 'Mrs W.K. Clifford', submitted excerpts from her novel *Love-Letters of a Worldly Woman*. She went to great lengths to ensure that her daughter, the poet Ethel Clifford, was also included, sending three letters about her, along with an extract of her work, to Princess Marie Louise.

Poems were also contributed by Alice Meynell, Margaret L. Woods, A. Mary F. Robinson and Pamela Grey, second wife of Edward Grey, 1st Viscount of Fallodon, and one of the famous Wyndham sisters (see page 32). Clemence Dane is the only female playwright to be represented in the Library. She copied out extracts from her well received play *Will Shakespeare*.

The majority of the contributions sent to the Dolls' House Library by women were extracts from novels, the authors tending to submit passages from their most popular works. Mary Cholmondeley copied out the closing words of her most successful novel *Red Pottage*, which had been criticised for being immoral on its first publication in 1899. Elinor Mordaunt also made a selection from her most popular book, *The Garden of Contentment*. Emphasising its success, she noted on her manuscript's title page the numerous dates of her novel's reprints.

A selection of books by women writers featured in the Dolls' House Library (from left to right):

Ethel M. Dell (1881–1939)
From 'The Bars of Iron', 1922
RCIN 1171490

Winifred Graham (1873–1950)
Royal Lovers, 1922
RCIN 1171414

Lucy Clifford (1846–1929)
Love-Letters of a Worldly Woman, 1922
RCIN 1171326

Beatrice Harraden (1864–1936)

Failure and Success, 1922

RCIN 1171469

Dame Ethel Smyth (1858–1944)

*The Empress Eugénie: from
'Streaks of Life'*, c.1922

RCIN 1171427

Clemence Dane (1888–1965)

*Some Songs and Sayings from
'Will Shakespeare'*, 1922

RCIN 1171515

Alice Meynell (1847–1922)

Poems, 1922

RCIN 1171431

Anne Douglas Sedgwick
(1873–1935)

From 'The Shadow of Life', 1922

RCIN 1171481

Vita Sackville-West (1892–1962)

A Note of Explanation, 1922

RCIN 1171551

Elizabeth von Arnim (1866–1941)

*How Mr Elliott became Engaged
to Anna-Felicitas*, 1922

RCIN 1171408

Pamela Tennant (later Viscountess Grey of Fallodon)
sits in the centre between her sisters, Madeline
Adeane and Lady Elcho (Mary Constance Charteris,
later Countess of Wemyss)

John Singer Sargent (1856–1925)

*The Wyndham Sisters: Lady Elcho, Mrs. Adeane,
and Mrs. Tennant*, 1899, oil on canvas

Metropolitan Museum of Art, New York

27. 67

The romantic novelist Ethel M. Dell submitted extracts from three of her bestsellers, *The Knave of Diamonds, The Bars of Iron* and *The Hundredth Chance*, while Elizabeth von Arnim made her contribution, an excerpt from her book *Christopher and Columbus*, under one of her pen-names, 'the Author of "Elizabeth & her German Garden"', the title of her first success. The philosopher, novelist and, at times, controversial feminist writer May Sinclair sent in an extract from her soon-to-be-published novel *Arnold Waterlow* (which at that time she was calling *Arnold Bywater*) along with two powerful poems about childhood, 'Fright' and 'Visionary', which had been published in 1920. 'Rita', a pseudonym of Eliza Humphreys, also contributed work in the process of being published: a passage from her novel *The Road to Anywhere*.

Original contributions came from Vita Sackville-West (whose manuscript about a ghost living in the Dolls' House is discussed on page 42) and Winifred Graham, who wrote *Royal Lovers* for the miniature library. In this story about a princess who resignedly decides to accept her next proposal for the good of the state, an initially cold relationship turns to passionate love after her prince dreams they encounter a dolls' house together. Una L. Silberrad, who wrote essays on women's equality and a novel in which she explored the possibility of a woman prime minister, contributed two articles. One, 'A Little Book of Wisdom', was original to the Dolls' House. E.M. Delafield, who wrote the popular *Diary of a Provincial Lady*,

'The old Colonel choked, turned aside, and to the amazement of everyone present, broke down and cried like a child.'

Very well: but what would have happened if that convenient space, and the new heading of Chapter V, hadn't been there?

They'd have to go on somehow.

The Colonel, for one, would have had to find a pocket-handkerchief . . .

E.M. Delafield, from her Dolls' House Library book, *Anti-Climax*

H. M. Bateman.

The trend towards female emancipation is depicted in the Dolls' House Library's portfolios:
Henry Mayo Bateman (1887–1970)
The Growth of Woman, 1922, pen and ink
RCIN 926808

submitted an amusing original essay called *Anti-Climax*, later published in a longer form, about the difference between novels, where climactic situations culminate with the chapter ending, and real life, where people have to deal with the consequences. 'Life is so inartistic', she writes.

The Dolls' House Library even contains a *History of Woman*, written by W.L. George. In his letter to Princess Marie Louise enclosing his little book he informed her that it summarised work shortly to be published serially in *The Fortnightly Review*. That would be 50,000 words, he told her, and his Dolls' House book only 335. However, he thought she would find it fairly complete.

Although in his miniature book he mainly writes of women as wives, he concedes that the nineteenth century saw them become novelists, scientists and politicians. He ends his history in February 1923 with some women having gained the vote and, he claims, equal access to professions as men. Optimistically, he concludes that a woman 'is free: her future lies in her own hands'.

'PLEASE DO NOT THINK I AM COMPLAINING, BECAUSE IT WAS ALL JOY'

Collecting the Manuscripts

· · · · · · · · · · ·

THE IDEA OF ASKING AUTHORS TO CONTRIBUTE miniature manuscripts originated with Sir Edwin Lutyens, the Dolls' House architect. 'Books are likely to give food for thought', he wrote to Princess Marie Louise in September 1921, in one of his numerous letters to her about the project. Their original plan had been to have small-scale copies of the classics printed specially. Lutyens had received a cost estimate for this, of £600 per book (today the equivalent to some £18,000 each). 'Dollyluyah!' he exclaims in his letter, 'too wild for words'. They must be content with miniature printed books already available, and, the idea seems to come to him as he writes, with asking authors to write in manuscript: 'a short story by Barrie would be fun'.

Soon afterwards, letters began to arrive in the hands of British and Irish writers. At the start of the project, these were sent by Leslie Chaundy, a London bookseller engaged as an agent by the Dolls' House scheme. His work was soon taken on by Princess Marie Louise herself, assisted by E.V. Lucas. 'I hope you will be willing to contribute a little book', Lucas's draft of the letter read. Writers were asked either for passages of what they had already published, or, preferably, something original. Those who were primarily known as poets were asked to make special selections of their works.

How the authors were chosen is a little unclear, but lists of writers in literary guides and of members of writers' societies were probably drawn upon. Some of the contributors seem to have been selected based on whom Lucas, Princess Marie Louise, Lutyens and Chaundy knew or could think of.

Walter Benington (1872–1936) for Elliott & Fry
E. V. Lucas, c.1930, chlorobromide print
National Portrait Gallery, London
NPG X94127

You have doubtless heard that a number of artists authors craftsmen & others have conspired to present to the Queen a Dolls House, or model residence in miniature, in which every thing that one would find in a King's Palace to-day is reproduced with minute accuracy so that it will have great historical value in the future. For the Library little books in the autograph of their writers are being prepared & will be specially bound. May I ask if you will be so good as to contribute one of these; and I venture to suggest that one of your delightful ghost stories ('The Haunted Dolls House'?) would be peculiarly appropriate. I enclose a little blank book for the purpose.

E.V. Lucas, draft letter to M.R. James, a version of which was sent to James by Princess Marie Louise in 1922
RA VIC/ADD/A/18/ML/2/1K-1L

The prolific writer Edward Verrall Lucas, always known as 'E.V.', was crucial to the formation of the Dolls' House Library's collections. The archive of correspondence on the Dolls' House includes many of his draft letters to writers and artists that Princess Marie Louise then copied and sent. Their work together brought them close.

'I may say that E.V. Lucas contributed a great deal to my life', the Princess wrote in her memoirs, 'our mutual friendship was, I think, as precious to him as it was to me.' Lutyens was also close to Lucas. 'I dined with E.V. last night', Lutyens wrote hurriedly to Princess Marie Louise in September 1922, '& didnt get to bed till .... best left untold?'

Lucas was well connected in literary circles, and many of the writers invited to contribute to the Dolls' House Library belonged to his extensive network. He wrote for the popular satirical magazine *Punch*, so it was natural for him to commission Owen Seaman, the Editor,

The literary cricket team at E.V. Lucas's daughter Audrey's school in 1913. E.V. Lucas is in the middle row, second from the right. Other Dolls' House authors pictured on the team are Harry Graham, on the top row, second from the right, and A.A. Milne, Maurice Hewlett and Sir J.M. Barrie, who are the first three on the left on the middle row

and fellow *Punch* contributors A.A. Milne and Fougasse. Lucas also had connections through a love of cricket, and was on *Peter Pan* writer Sir J.M. Barrie's cricket team. Other team members among the Dolls' House Library contributors were Sir Arthur Conan Doyle, Harry Graham, Maurice Hewlett and, again, A.A. Milne. Lucas was described by Milne in the eulogy he wrote on Lucas's

death in 1938 as 'the writer most loved as a man by other writers'.

In some cases when Lucas drafted letters for the Princess to send to potential contributors, he gave particular suggestions for Dolls' House books. To M.R. James he wrote: 'I venture to suggest that one of your delightful ghost stories ("The Haunted Dolls House"?) would be peculiarly appropriate';

'The school' he said 'was divided into two halves … at a given signal both sides charged for it, and' – this is the point I particularly admire – 'there were no rules.' No rules! Think of it, and contrast it with the perpetual blowing of the referee's whistle on a football ground now.

Horace G. Hutchinson, recounting a tale of the first ever rugby match, from his Dolls' House Library book, *A Manual of Games*

Below: Sketch by Sir Edwin Lutyens of himself kneeling before Gertrude Jekyll, *c.*1896

and critic Desmond MacCarthy that he write a little manual on English literature for dolls was even more unsuccessful. Despite originally responding with an enthusiastic letter promising a 'Lilliputian' book of literary criticism, MacCarthy ultimately did not participate at all.

Sir Edwin Lutyens also secured the contributions of several authors, although ostensibly he was not directly involved in the day-to-day administration of forming the Dolls' House Library's collection. Through him writers professed their desire to contribute, or agreed to do so following his persuasion.

while Horace G. Hutchinson, who wrote about sport, was asked for a manual on games for the dolls. He responded with just that, writing about golf, cricket and tennis, and even recounting a conversation with a man who was part of the first ever rugby match in 1850.

But authors did not always follow the directions Lucas gave them. The suggestion to the political journalist Sir Henry Lucy (who wrote in *Punch* as 'Toby, MP') that he contribute coverage of a debate in the Dolls' House of Commons went unmet, with Lucy instead copying something from his memoirs. Lucas's request to the reviewer

Above: The Dolls' House Garden, designed by Gertrude Jekyll, completed 1924

Right: Gertrude Jekyll (1843–1932)
The Garden, 1922
RCIN 1171449

One such was the famous garden designer and writer Gertrude Jekyll, Lutyens' friend and collaborator from the very beginning of his career. As well as designing the Dolls' House's garden, which contains trees made from real twigs and delicate model flowers, butterflies and even a miniscule snail, she wrote an introduction to gardening especially for the Library.

Gertrude Jekyll's sister-in-law Dame Agnes Jekyll, also good friends with Lutyens, likewise wrote for the

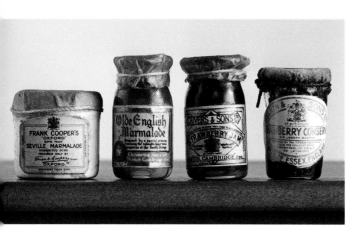

Miniature jars of marmalade and jam from
the Dolls' House Stores, collected 1921–4

RCINs 231077, 230294, 230293, 230622

Dolls' House Library alongside being
involved in the House more generally.
She provided a recipe book, as well as
collecting together miniature items for
the stores, including six tins of toffees,
18 jars of marmalade and 48 tiny boxes
of chocolates.

    Sir J.M. Barrie, most famous now
as the writer of *Peter Pan*, was also
close to Lutyens. Although he was a
good friend and cricketing team mate
of E.V. Lucas, it was Lutyens who
originally approached him when he first
thought of the idea of commissioning
manuscripts for the Library. 'I spoke to
Barrie last night who is agreeable &
willing', he wrote to Princess Marie
Louise in November 1921, soon after
the plan to ask authors for manuscripts
had been agreed. They had been
friends for years, and Lutyens designed

Letter from Sir J.M. Barrie to
Princess Marie Louise, 17 March 1922

RA VIC/ADD/A/18/ML/22

stage sets for him, including that for *Peter Pan* in 1904. The architect is even credited with suggesting the character of 'Nana', the children's dog in the well-loved play. This connection is celebrated in the Dolls' House by a miniature toy theatre in the Day Nursery, which has a revolving stage revealing three sets from *Peter Pan*.

Barrie's submission was late, and he finally returned his booklet to the organisers with apologies for this, explaining that it was 'filled

Above: W. Wilkinson and T. Hembrow

Miniature toy theatre, 1924, wood, paper and silk

RCIN 230227

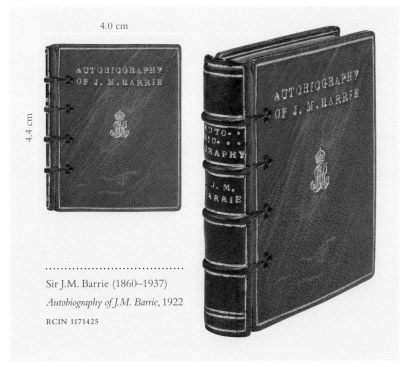

4.0 cm

4.4 cm

Sir J.M. Barrie (1860–1937)

Autobiography of J.M. Barrie, 1922

RCIN 1171425

CHAPTER 1

At six 'twas thus I wrote my name,
James Barrie

CHAPTER 2

At twelve it was not quite the same,
James M. Barrie

*Sir J.M. Barrie, from his Dolls' House Library book,
Autobiography of J.M. Barrie*

up as far as my failing fancy allows'. He entitled it *Autobiography*, and it is the story of his life told through his changing signature.

Another contributor suggested to Princess Marie Louise and Lucas by Lutyens was his sister Mary Lutyens, a relatively obscure author who published under her married name, Mrs George Wemyss. The book she wrote for the Dolls' House Library, *White's Lane*, is a moving tale about a mother who loses her sons in the First World War.

Connection with Lutyens brought two further highlights to the Library: contributions from Vita Sackville-West and her husband, Harold Nicolson. They knew Lutyens through Vita's mother, Lady Sackville, who was his particularly close friend; indeed, both their families believed they were lovers. Lady Sackville donated

some printed books to the Dolls' House and funded an album of miniature stamps for the Library; appropriately, as King George V was known to be a keen stamp collector.

Vita Sackville-West's contribution, *A Note of Explanation*, is one of the few works set in Queen Mary's Dolls' House itself. A ghost establishes herself in the House where she sleeps in a different room every night and, despite having the inconvenience of being stuck in the lift for an afternoon, enjoys making use of all the modern inventions with which it is equipped, leaving lights on, baths full and the Dolls' House guardians perplexed. Sackville-West's friendship with Lutyens meant that she could refer in her little book to aspects of the House that others, further removed from the architect, would not have been privy to before it was exhibited. She mentioned the painted bedrooms, the malachite bath with silver taps and, playfully, the big spectacles worn by the House's architect.

Sackville-West's husband, Harold Nicolson, would later become a well-known biographer, commissioned to write the official biography of King George V, but in the early 1920s he was working in the Foreign Office and had only just started his literary career. He was not an obvious choice for inclusion in the Dolls' House Library, and indeed would not have been invited without

Lutyens' intervention: 'Harold Nicolson …
still clamours to be allowed to write a book',
Lutyens wrote to Princess Marie Louise from
Delhi in October 1922 in his characteristic
rushed scrawl; 'E.V.L[ucas] said let it slide, but
it wont. Do you think he might? It would
cause him & his wife Mrs N. to purr.'

Nicolson's contribution, *The Detail of
Biography*, notes changing styles in the writing
of biographies. Lamenting the gaps in records
that the biographer of his day has to bridge,
he admits feeling envious of his counterpart
writing in 2023, who will be able to use
Queen Mary's Dolls' House to illuminate the
life of the English gentleman of 1923.

> There was, for instance, the Doll's-
> house ghost, because naturally the
> Doll's-house was haunted, being a
> completely appointed house, and all
> really nice houses being haunted, thick
> and variously, if only by the vows of
> love that have been exchanged there
> (and where they survive unbroken), or
> by the songs that have been sung there
> out of a happy heart.
>
> Vita Sackville-West, from her Dolls' House
> Library book, *A Note of Explanation*

....
Vita Sackville-West (1892–1962)

A Note of Explanation, 1922

RCIN 1171551

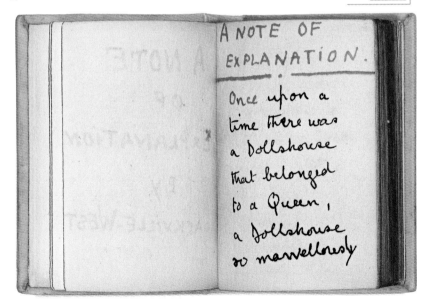

....
Harold Nicolson and Vita Sackville-
West in her writing room in the Tower
at Sissinghurst Castle, Kent, 1932
National Trust Images

Lutyens' interventions were not always so successful. He wrote to Princess Marie Louise in June 1922 that Arthur Clutton-Brock, an essayist, would write for the Dolls' House: 'he says it will be dull but is ever there a library without dull books?'. The Princess duly invited Clutton-Brock to contribute. He replied awkwardly that though he was flattered by the request he could not think of anything to write in the little book that would be worthy of the occasion, and that he had not thought that Lutyens seriously wished him to do it.

Lists amongst the Dolls' House papers in the Royal Archives show which writers the organisers planned to invite. By no means all of those listed were eventually represented in the miniature library. Among these are H.G. Wells, Marie Corelli and Lady Gregory, but it is unclear whether in the end they were not invited, or they were, but refused. Perhaps H.G. Wells was excluded, or excluded himself, on consideration of his 1901 book *Anticipations*, which discussed republics replacing monarchies. Another list in the Royal Archives records authors who were invited but did not respond, including W.B. Yeats and D.H. Lawrence.

There is a short, probably incomplete, list of writers who refused. Lord Rosebery, who had been Prime Minister from 1894 to 1895, declined, despite, as Princess Marie Louise records in her autobiography, having gallantly come to her aid before when, aged 15, she had burst into tears after another man had looked her up and down, then refused to take her in to dinner. John Masefield, who would in 1930 become Poet Laureate, also declined his invitation, as did the Modernist writer Virginia Woolf, who had yet to meet and form a relationship with Dolls'-House-scheme-champion Vita Sackville-West. Woolf mentioned to her friend Janet Case that she felt the invitation was a compliment, but her husband persuaded her not to take part.

The refusal of George Bernard Shaw particularly irritated the Princess: she recalls in her memoirs that he wrote in a very rude manner. 'His letter was not even amusing … not worthy of one who claimed, as he did, to be a man of genius.' Perhaps because of his refusal, George Bernard Shaw was a figure of fun for several of the writers contributing to the Dolls' House Library. C.H. Collins Baker, in *Art Seen through Doll Eyes*, added pretend publishers' adverts to the end of his miniature book, including one for 'The Art of Boring: how to empty a Theatre. By G.B.S.'; while the playwright Sir Arthur Wing Pinero, in his Dolls' House book *Little Fables*, wrote of two oxen discussing Shaw's lack of patriotism. '"I hear Mr. Shaw is a vegetarian," … "Ah," said the first ox quickly, "I dare say the man is very much maligned."'

There are notable omissions even from preliminary lists of potential contributors. Leading writers such as T.S. Eliot, James Joyce, Jerome K. Jerome, E.M. Forster, Ezra Pound,

Ford Madox Ford and P.G. Wodehouse all might have been invited, but they do not appear to have been. Some of those missing were prominent in the Modernist literary movement and perhaps were incompatible with the miniature library's more middlebrow tone. The documentation left by the project is unclear on whether the conventional nature of the collection of manuscripts was deliberate, in spite of the oft-stated aim that it was to be representative, or was merely an unintended result of a combination of the refusals of certain authors and the tastes of the organisers.

Popular children's authors also seem to have been excluded. Edith Nesbit, Eleanor Farjeon, Beatrix Potter and Frances Hodgson Burnett would surely have been ideal for a project such as the Dolls' House Library, but their omission makes it clear that the Dolls' House was not for children.

⇨◆⇦

Once writers had received their invitations and agreed to contribute, they were sent tiny booklets. These they were to fill in using their smallest handwriting and send back to the organisers to be beautifully bound. If it was not possible for them to write so small, they were to provide material which would be transcribed professionally, which they should then sign.

Queen Mary's copies of A.C. Benson (1862–1925) and Sir Lawrence Weaver (1876–1930) (eds), *The Book of the Queen's Dolls' House*, 1924, and E.V. Lucas (1868–1938) (ed.), *The Book of the Queen's Dolls' House Library*, 1924 (RCINs 1080370–1), with a selection of miniature manuscripts

In summer 1923, even though the majority of the little booklets had been returned, Princess Marie Louise wrote to all the Dolls' House Library manuscript contributors again: the organisers had decided on a publication that would catalogue the books of the Library and reproduce much of their contents, concentrating in particular on writing composed specially for the Dolls' House and poems selected into arrangements uniquely for the purpose. E.V. Lucas was to edit this volume, called *The Book of the Queen's Dolls' House Library*. Published in 1924 to coincide with the display of the Dolls' House at the British Empire Exhibition, it was produced along with *The Book of the Queen's Dolls' House*, which described the whole of the rest of the House and Garden.

The Princess approached the authors to request permission to reproduce their work in this catalogue. Most were delighted to be involved, although keen to see proofs, fearing mistakes made in the copying of their minute, often rather unclear, handwriting. A few, like F.W. Bain, hesitated: they had not believed anyone would ever read their doll manuscripts. Bain wrote to the publisher to add another line to his story, which he felt greatly improved it, and confided modestly, 'if I had known that it was to have been honoured with print, I could easily have made it much better'.

Throughout the summer of 1922, Princess Marie Louise, with Lucas's guidance, also wrote to hundreds of British and Irish artists asking them to contribute a small drawing, watercolour or print, just 1 by 1½ inches (2.5 by 3.8 cm), for inclusion in miniature portfolios.

Princess Marie Louise estimated that she wrote more than 2,000 letters in the course of her work on the Dolls' House, 'though please do not think I am complaining, because it was all joy', she explained in her memoirs. While, as Lutyens foresaw, a short story by Barrie is indeed fun, the wealth of correspondence and documentation about the Dolls' House Library kept in the Royal Archives is testament to the great efforts made by Lucas, Lutyens and the Princess in its organisation.

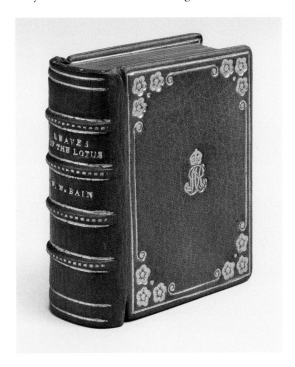

F.W. Bain (1863–1940)

Leaves of the Lotus, 1922

RCIN 1171441

'IT IS VERY BADLY WRITTEN, & I HOPE IT WILL NOT BE USED'

Problems faced by the organisers and contributors

By the end of December 1922 most of the manuscripts had been received. The writers had risen to the challenge with amusement and ingenuity, although the task had not been easy, and the process of organising contributions to the Dolls' House Library had not always gone smoothly.

The administrator Leslie Chaundy had problems co-ordinating the commissioning of writers and liaising with the bookbinders. Maurice Hewlett, W.H. Davies and Sir Arthur Quiller-Couch (who published as 'Q') all claimed not to have had any communication from Chaundy in their responses to the Princess's letters chasing late contributions, which she sent in March 1922. Chaundy then appears to have got some of the books bound without the oversight of Princess Marie Louise, following which, in June 1922, Sir Edwin Lutyens wrote to the Princess fearing that she was so annoyed with the agent she had caught 'Chaundyitis'. Soon afterwards, Chaundy's involvement appears to have ended, and Princess Marie Louise and

E.V. Lucas took on the bulk of the administrative work themselves.

One error that was not uncovered until after the project was completed was due to a mix-up with names. Joseph Pennell, a London bookbinder, on receiving an invitation asking him to contribute, duly sent in a miniature book of uninspired maxims. However, it was to the American author and illustrator also named Joseph Pennell that a letter of thanks was sent by Queen Mary on completion of the Dolls' House in 1924. This latter Pennell had lived in Britain for many years and was married to the author Elizabeth Robins Pennell (not to be confused with Dolls' House contributor Elizabeth Robins), with whom he collaborated on a number of publications. No doubt he was the intended recipient of the invitation rather than the bookbinder. He was understandably confused, and in newspaper articles detailing the muddle he describes the maxims attributed to him as 'drivel'. Lucas was approached for comment and remarked

From the Dolls' House Library's portfolios:
Christopher Richard Wynne Nevinson (1889–1946)
Rooftops and Mountains, c.1922, pen and ink
RCIN 927220

mischievously, 'they are pretty bad. That
convinced me that he wrote them'.

Responding to the invitation was not
necessarily straightforward for the writers
and artists. For one thing, the Princess's
handwriting could be very difficult to read.
The artist Christopher Richard Wynne
Nevinson replied to the request made to him
to contribute a drawing with an explanation
that (despite also being a journalist) he never
reads the papers so has not heard of any dolls'
house. As he could not read the signature

on the letter sent to him, he did not know
to whom he was writing in response. 'I have
had to stick the signature on to the envelope,
I could think of nothing else as a solution',
he wrote. 'I hope you won't think me rude.'

Others found that addressing a princess
could be a cause of anxiety. Ethel Clifford,
who contributed poems selected from two of
her published collections, began her response
to Princess Marie Louise, 'Dear Madam, Do
Please forgive me if that is the wrong way to
begin. There is no-one at hand to consult', and
panicked when it came to ending her letter:

Envelope of a letter from Christopher
Richard Wynne Nevinson to Princess
Marie Louise, 9 July 1922
RA VIC/ADD/A/18/ML/12B/22B

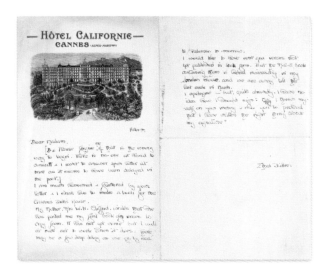

Letter from Ethel Dilke (the married name of Ethel Clifford) to Princess Marie Louise, 8 February 1923 (?)

RA VIC/ADD/A/18/ML/12A/6A

'I apologise – but, quite absurdly, I have no idea how I should sign: May I throw myself on your mercy & ask you to pretend that I have written the right thing above my signature?'

⬥

'You do not notify when you expect these little books to be returned and everyone who writes books is endowed with the gift of procrastination', the journalist Clement Shorter, whose offering was an account of the little books the Brontë sisters wrote when they were children, warned the Princess on receipt of her invitation. Delays in receiving contributions were indeed something with which the organisers of the Dolls' House Library had to contend. Some authors found that the little book took a conversely long time to write. The architect Sir Reginald Blomfield took seven months to write his contribution, a description of the palatial house of the fictional Marquis of Carabas. Blomfield wrote this specially for the Dolls' House, though he pretended he had edited it from a rare manuscript of fairy stories by the French author Charles Perrault.

Illness held back some authors. W.E. Norris, aged 75 in 1922, contributed a condensed version of his short story *A Peasant of Lorraine* rather than anything new because, as he confided in Princess Marie Louise, he had been incapable of much exertion and had only recently been allowed out of bed. Illness also troubled novelist and playwright Clemence Dane, whose submission, songs from her play *Will Shakespeare*, was sent late: she explained in her accompanying letter that she had been ill for a month and found writing to be shaky and difficult.

Some delays were less excusable. The poet A. Mary F. Robinson, who submitted 24 poems, admitted to the Princess that she 'began writing in the tiny volume with much zest and zeal, and then – called away by urgent work from this delightful play – put the fairy-like thing in a drawer and quite forgot it'.

Deciding what to contribute to the Dolls' House could be difficult, and inspiration did not always strike. Lucy Clifford explained this to Princess Marie Louise in one of several letters she sent about the project. When it comes to composing something new, she wrote, 'one is <u>so</u> at the mercy of something <u>in</u> one'. As her 'poor brain' refused to think of anything, she submitted extracts from her novel *Love-Letters of a Worldly Woman*, a book which, she claimed, contains many things from her heart and soul. Ann Douglas Sedgwick, in a similar predicament, also contributed work to which she felt particularly close. She chose an extract from her novel *The Passage of Life*, which, she wrote in a letter to the Princess, she felt very fond of, plus it seemed more suitable than anything she could think of on the spur of the moment.

Ethel M. Dell originally responded to her invitation by asking Princess Marie Louise to make any selection she liked from her works: she felt unable to contribute anything original, not feeling 'artistically equal' to such a task. On receiving encouragement she filled in her little book with extracts from three of her published novels. Despite being described by Lucas in his *The Book of the Queen's Dolls' House Library* as 'the most popular English writer of the present day', she felt her attempt was poor and unworthy, and expressed surprise to the Princess that her work was considered to be of sufficient importance to be included in the collection.

For some potential contributors, the problem of originality was insurmountable. Augustine Birrell, politician and author, confided in the Princess, 'I am really much perturbed at not being able to do what you ask. But the fact is that my Imagination, once active enough, is now <u>extinct</u> … It simply can't be done.' He considered contributing something he had already published, but felt that would be shameful.

If writers did come up with something unique for the Dolls' House, there could then be difficulties if they wanted to make it available elsewhere before the House was presented to the public. After he had submitted his miniature manuscript in summer 1922, W. Somerset Maugham sent a copy of it to *Pearson's Magazine* for publication. This caused some upset amongst the Library organisers, with Lutyens threatening to refuse to allow the book to remain in the Dolls' House. As Maugham was contractually obliged to go ahead with publication, Princess Marie Louise wrote to the editor of the magazine to mediate,

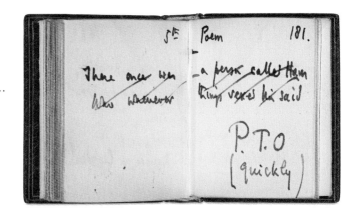

. . . .

Jokingly crossing out the
first lines of a limerick that
risked becoming too rude.
E.F. Benson (1867–1940)

Poems, 1922

RCIN 1171429

and a compromise was reached whereby the
magazine agreed not to mention for what
reason the story was written. Its introduction
to the piece, printed in December 1922,
reads mysteriously: 'this delightful story was
written by Mr. Maugham for a very special
purpose, the nature of which we are not, at
the moment, permitted to disclose'.

The minute nature of the work daunted
many of the authors. James Owen Hannay,
who used the pseudonym 'George A.
Birmingham', thought his handwriting was
deplorable, and Lucy Clifford felt hers was
'lumbering'. Both asked their daughters to
transcribe their texts into the little books for
them. Others persisted. The adventure novelist
Stanley J. Weyman's first attempt at writing a
tale from his short-story collection *In Kings'
Byways* into the little booklet provided him
was unsightly, he confessed to Princess Marie
Louise, and he was very ill-satisfied with it. He
requested another blank booklet be sent to
him and felt that his second attempt was, with
all its drawbacks, a little more legible.

Eyesight hindered several writers
including Thomas Hardy, who explained
to the Princess that a weakness of the eyes
prevented him from copying out his poems
clearly, and Ethel Clifford, who could only
write three pages a day, the small writing
tried her eyes so. The Poet Laureate Robert
Bridges, who had held the position since
1913, at first declined the invitation to
contribute, informing Leslie Chaundy that
neither his hands nor his eyes were youthful
enough to carry out the miniature work
creditably, and 'that the thing was better not
done than done badly'. Princess Marie Louise
and Lucas intervened – they could not have a
doll royal library without an offering from the
Poet Laureate – and wrote again to persuade
him. Bridges made another attempt, selecting
22 of his poems and writing out many of them
himself. His wife Monica Bridges, an expert
calligrapher who had published an influential
manual on handwriting, inscribed the rest.

It could be difficult to gauge how long
a story would need to be to fill up the little

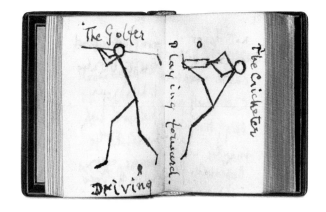

....

Horace G. Hutchinson
(1859–1932)

A Manual of Games, 1922

RCIN 1171496

blank booklets. The playwright Edward Knoblock apologised to Princess Marie Louise for not filling the entire volume sent to him. He had been so afraid of making his contribution too long that, when he came to copying it into the miniature book, he found that he had erred the other way. While he added decorative flourishes to bulk out his work, G.K. Chesterton, facing a similar problem, filled up the remainder of his booklet with 30 pages of fake, satirical reviews. Fellow writers George Bernard Shaw and Sir J.M. Barrie are pretend reviewers, along with Sigmund Freud, Albert Einstein, the President of the United States and the Pope.

Occasionally writers made mistakes in their little booklets. Some accidentally turned over two of the tiny pages at once when writing them, leaving blanks. A few used pictures to fill the gaps: Max Pemberton asked a friend to draw his story's main character on the pages he had skipped, while Horace G. Hutchinson drew stick figures of a cricketer and a golfer into his *Manual of Games*. Crossed-out words can be found throughout the books, although the two pages with lines through in E.F. Benson's contribution are a deliberate joke.

With all these problems and pitfalls, it is perhaps not surprising that several of the writers professed a lack of confidence in their submissions to the Dolls' House Library. Rose Macaulay contributed her book of two poems, 'The Alien' and 'The Thief', to Princess Marie Louise with the modest comment 'it is very badly written, & I hope it will not be used'. Maurice Baring confided that his poem *Elegy on the Death of Juliet's Owl* was 'as neatly as I could write (I am afraid it is rather badly done)', while Clement Shorter wrote 'I send you my very feeble contribution but I shall not be hurt if it is burnt & not bound'. Their modesty is misplaced. Despite various challenges, the majority of the manuscripts given to the Library are well-chosen pieces, often presented with skilful handwriting and delicate illustrations.

'EVERY TASTE HAS BEEN CONSIDERED'

The Contents of the Manuscripts

. . . .

THE MANUSCRIPTS CONTRIBUTED TO the Dolls' House are, with one or two exceptions, around 4 cm high. They are all, however, of different thicknesses, reflecting not just the amount written in them, but the size of the handwriting used. Some of the books are just a hundred words or fewer, whereas others are close to 5,000. The shorter books tend to have been bound in limp vellum – specially treated calf or sheep skin, cream in colour – their covers less rigid than those on the thicker books, which are more colourful. Most have gilded page edges and gold-tooled leather bindings, which are an astonishing display of the skill of those who bound them.

The handwriting in the manuscripts varies as much as the subject matter, but most of the books show that the contributors were attempting to write neatly, with some even writing calligraphically. The art of calligraphy was often part of education, and had recently experienced a revival during the Arts and Crafts movement, so it is not surprising that some of the writers possessed elements of the skill.

Many of the manuscripts have carefully laid-out title pages, marked-up chapter headings and page numbers as if they were printed books, and some also contain lists of contents, indexes, footnotes for references and errata pages for noting mistakes, just as if they were published versions. Hilaire Belloc went so far as to add a spurious publishing statement to his book, pretending it was produced by the firm 'Lyfreely and Cozen'.

St John Lucas and A. Mary F. Robinson, who both submitted poems, were unusual in

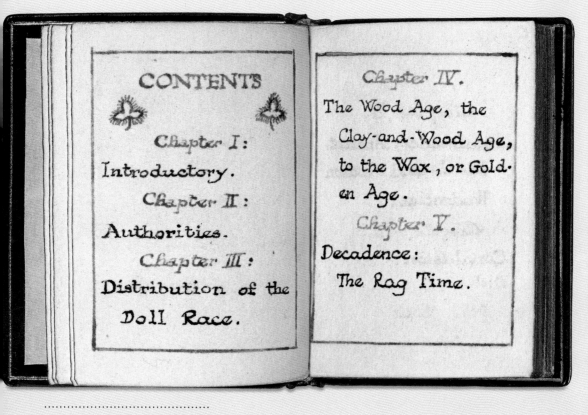

CONTENTS

Sir E. Denison Ross (1871–1940)

An Outline of Dollery, by a Doll, 1923

RCIN 1171524

writing their contributions into their booklets sideways, and W.H. Davies copied out his short poem 'Thunderstorms' with one or two words written diagonally across each page. In his striking layout his words are more impactful than in an ordinary printed copy of his poem. E.F. Benson wrote his poems across each double-page opening in his booklet (see page 52). In a postscript to the preface of his manuscript, he noted that 'these poems must be read right across the two pages…. They can be read first down one page & then the other, but it is no good doing that as they won't mean anything.'

While most of the authors made a good attempt to lay out their books well and write in tiny handwriting, some, such as the popular novelist E. Phillips Oppenheim who sent in an account of Villa Deveron, his idyllic new home on the French Riviera, did not moderate their style. He wrote one word per line in his little book, and only four or five words to a page. Sir H. Rider Haggard feared that his natural

Letter from Sir H. Rider Haggard to Princess Marie Louise, 3 April 1922

RA VIC/ADD/A/18/ML/194

way of writing was little suited to the Dolls' House, but told Princess Marie Louise that he had done his best. His contribution is the last passage from his agricultural diary of 1898, *A Farmer's Year*. While his writing begins rather small, at about 20 words per page, it gets bigger and bigger throughout his book until by the end he only manages to fit in six words.

Several of the contributors, unable to write out their books themselves due to age, illness or poor eyesight, left the task to trained calligraphers. Most of these, such as A.J. Ketley who beautifully inscribed Thomas Hardy's manuscript (see page 66), worked for the bookbinders Sangorski & Sutcliffe.

....

Joseph Conrad (1857–1924)
The Nursery of the Craft, 1922
RCIN 1171555

The calligraphers penned the selections of works made by poets and authors in gold and coloured inks, some even adding illustrations, like the unknown calligrapher working for Sangorski & Sutcliffe who wrote out Joseph Conrad's contribution.

Some professional calligraphers contributed work in their own right. Graily Hewitt, one of the foremost calligraphers of the day, was invited to send in a drawing or watercolour for the Dolls' House Library art portfolios. He responded instead with a small

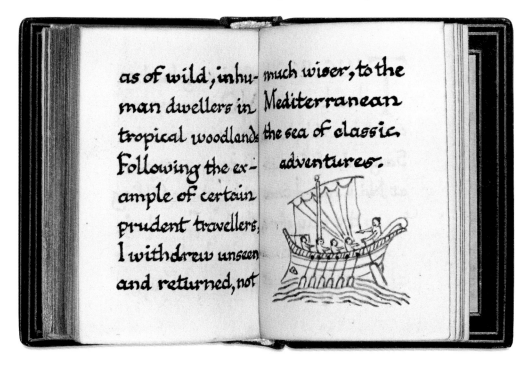

Left: Charles Kingsley
(1819–75)

Calligraphy by Graily
Hewitt (1864–1952)

The Prettiest Doll, 1922,
manuscript on vellum

RCIN 1171108

Opposite: William
Blake (1757–1827)

Calligraphy by Doris
M. Lee (active 1923)

Songs of Innocence, 1923,
manuscript on vellum

RCIN 1171405

exceptionally so. One of the most highly illustrated books contributed to the Dolls' House is a birthday book made by Lady Lloyd of Bronwydd Castle in Cardiganshire, Wales. No birthdays are recorded in the book, but Katherine Lloyd opened each month with a full-page illustration of either a seasonal sport or a palace or castle. A figure toboggans headfirst down a snowy hill for January, while yachts sail past a lighthouse for July. Royal residences St James's Palace, Balmoral and Windsor Castle are all depicted (see pages 60–61). Lady Lloyd had previously created a larger copy, which King George V and Queen Mary both signed. The Queen reportedly greatly admired the book, and asked for a miniature version to be made for her Dolls' House.

It is not only hand-drawn works of art which adorn the Dolls' House manuscripts. George Williamson, an art historian, on finding himself consulted by several of the artists who had been asked to contribute

vellum book into which he had copied the poem 'I Once had a Sweet Little Doll, Dears' from Charles Kingsley's *The Water-Babies*. He explained in a letter to Princess Marie Louise that he was not a maker of pictures, but Her Doll Majesty would be in need of a vellum manuscript, in imitation of medieval books, to make her library collection complete. Calligrapher Doris M. Lee also sent in a book demonstrating her skill, copying out poems by William Blake in multi-coloured inks, decorating them in beautiful detail.

Many of the miniature books were illustrated by the writers – some

a miniature work to the project, wrote to Princess Marie Louise to ask if he, too, could submit something. He pasted into a little book a selection of specially reduced printed royal portraits, and alongside each he wrote details of the original painting. One of the reproductions he included is of a portrait miniature of Marie Antoinette, Queen of France. According to Williamson's commentary, the original miniature had once been thought to be of little value, and the governess who owned it let her charges keep it in their dolls' house. Apparently Queen Victoria visited the family, saw the

portrait in the dolls' house, and, recognising its importance, upset the children by commanding them to return it to their governess immediately.

Creating books for the Dolls' House was an opportunity to demonstrate an ability to write and illustrate on a miniature scale. The contributors' work is all the more remarkable for having been done on the assumption that only the Library's organisers would see it. Although E.V. Lucas put facsimiles of some of the pages in his catalogue, they do little justice to their intricate beauty. Together with the skilled bindings, the decorative contents of the

books demonstrate the care and delight with
which many of the writers entered into the
spirit of the Dolls' House Library project.

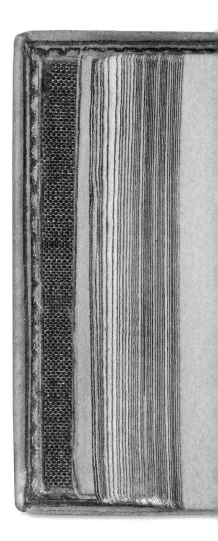

Perhaps even more noteworthy than the
bindings, handwriting and illustration of
the manuscripts is the snapshot the contents
of the books provide of British and Irish
literature, society and culture in the 1920s.
As Lucas claims in his introduction to the
miniature library in his edited catalogue, 'the
dolls, it will be seen, are not to be pitied when
a dull day drives them to the bookshelves, for
every taste has been considered'.

Subjects covered by the manuscripts
show that there were several broad themes
influencing what many of the writers
chose to copy out or invent for the scheme,
including the recent First World War and
the conceit that the Library was for dolls,
fairies or children. Unique contributions,
either written especially for the Dolls' House,
or unpublished at the point of submission,
are of great significance to the study of the
output of those who wrote them, as are the
collections of poems gathered together by
numerous poets into new arrangements not
found elsewhere. As a representation of the
work of British and Irish writers of the 1920s,
the Dolls' House Library remains unparalleled.

Windsor Castle
Katherine Lloyd (d. 1937)
*Birthday Book, c.*1924
RCIN 1171517

61

'POEMS ABRIDGED FOR DOLLS AND PRINCES'

Poetry in the Dolls' House Library

Some of the most revered poets of late Victorian Britain and Ireland, as well as those who were younger and more modern, were approached for contributions to the Dolls' House Library. They were asked to make new collections of their works specially for the occasion, summed up by Robert Graves in the title of his manuscript, *Poems: Abridged for Dolls and Princes*.

A highlight amongst the poetry in the Dolls' House Library is Rudyard Kipling's submission. Like many of the authors who contributed, he, while not primarily known as an artist, took the opportunity to decorate his work. He illustrated with delicate pen-and-ink drawings a selection of ten of his poems taken from books including *Just So Stories*, *Kim* and *Rewards and Fairies*. He adapted his handwriting and chose different decorative styles to reflect the themes and content of each poem. His manuscript begins with 'If', the poem's pages unembellished apart from an end flourish. 'The Way through the Woods', in this instance titled by Kipling

'The Road through the Woods', is also largely left plain, but opens with a full-page illustration showing trees with bare branches and a broken fence flanking a path. Kipling begins 'A Charm' with a sketch of a graveyard and ends it with a gnarled tree stump; while 'Eddi's Service' is illustrated throughout with Celtic designs twining around the words.

Although criticised then as well as now for his colonialist stance, Kipling received approbation for his manuscript. Princess Marie Louise wrote in her autobiography that the American book collector A.S.W. Rosenbach, on seeing Kipling's Dolls' House contribution, offered her a four-figure sum for it. 'Nothing doing', she told him, refusing to sell, 'it is the Queen's property'.

Opposite: Opening page of 'The Road through the Woods'

Rudyard Kipling (1865–1936)

Verses, 1922

RCIN 1171484

The Road
Through The
Woods

£1,000 then would be worth around £40,000 today, but as the bookbinder George Sutcliffe wrote to the Princess in March 1922, 'Mr. Kipling's manuscript is really priceless'.

Another well-known writer who contributed poetry to the Dolls' House Library was A.E. Housman, famed for his collection *A Shropshire Lad*. He was renowned for not allowing his work to be republished in anthologies, and E.V. Lucas had fallen foul of him in 1899 when he had included some of Housman's works in his compilation volume, *The Open Road*, without permission. Fortunately for the Dolls' House Library, Housman considered Princess Marie Louise 'my old, dear, and intimate friend', and at her request that he contribute, he selected, as he relayed to his publisher, poems of his that were 'the 12 shortest and simplest and least likely to fatigue the attention of dolls or members of the illustrious House of Hanover'. Seven of these were taken from *A Shropshire Lad*, and five from *Last Poems*.

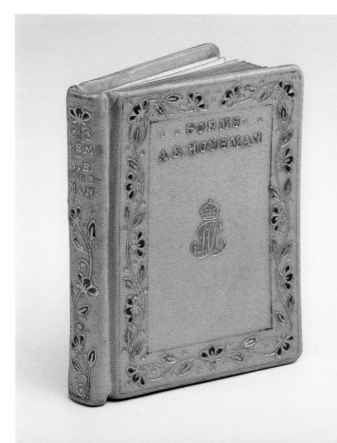

A.E. Housman (1859–1936)

*Poems, c.*1922

RCIN 1171451

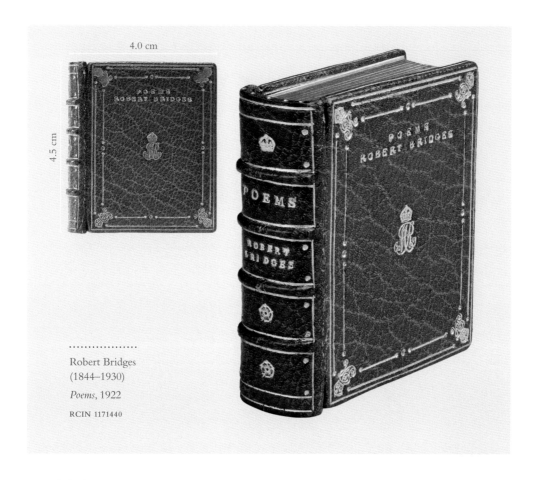

4.0 cm

4.5 cm

Robert Bridges
(1844–1930)
Poems, 1922
RCIN 1171440

While future Poet Laureate John Masefield refused to take part, the incumbent, Robert Bridges, after initially demurring due to his eyesight, submitted 22 poems that he had written between 1873 and 1920, taking them from his published collections.

The novelist and poet Thomas Hardy, much revered by his fellow writers in the 1920s, sent Princess Marie Louise a list of only three poems on her request for a contribution: 'The Oxen', 'When I Set Out for Lyonesse' and 'In Time of "the Breaking of Nations"'. She asked for more, and Hardy,

Left and below: Thomas Hardy (1840–1928)
Calligraphy by A.J. Ketley (active 1922–3)
Poems, 1922
RCIN 1171531

though admitting he felt uncertain of his choices, suggested another 14. The Princess selected most of them and had them copied into the tiny book by one of Sangorski & Sutcliffe's calligraphers, A.J. Ketley. On receiving it in order that he could sign his name, Hardy remarked that he was very much pleased: 'it makes one wish to have a whole library of such books!'.

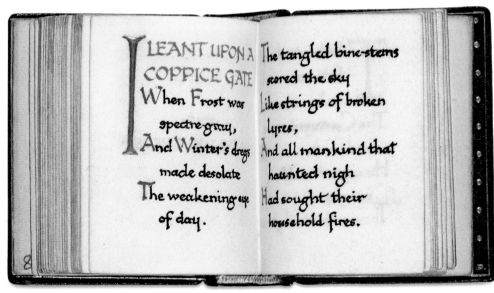

I LEANT UPON A COPPICE GATE
When Frost was spectre-gray,
And Winter's dregs made desolate
The weakening eye of day.

The tangled bine-stems scored the sky
Like strings of broken lyres,
And all mankind that haunted nigh
Had sought their household fires.

Another significant miniature volume of poetry contributed to the Dolls' House is by Edward Marsh, a civil servant who became an important patron of the arts. He edited the popular *Georgian Poetry* anthologies from 1912. (Here, 'Georgian' refers to Marsh's contemporaries – poets writing during the reign of King George V (r. 1910–36) – rather than to the times of the earlier kings named George.) Marsh published five volumes of *Georgian Poetry* over ten years, and through these introduced the general reader to modern poetry. For the Dolls' House Library, Marsh brought out a sixth volume, collecting together 27 poems and copying them out himself.

Marsh included poets not represented elsewhere in the miniature library. Some of these, such as Isaac Rosenberg and Rupert Brooke, had died in the First World War. Brooke, influential in the setting up of the *Georgian Poetry* series, was one of the most

renowned poets of the early years of the war, and his sonnet 'The Soldier', included in Marsh's Dolls' House contribution, is one of the most famous of war poems. Other poets in Marsh's manuscript volume did not have their

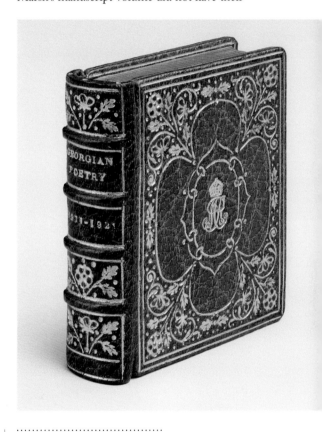

Edward Marsh (1872–1953)
Georgian Poetry 1911–1921, 1922
RCIN 1171412

If I should die, think only this of me:
That there's some corner of a foreign field
That is forever England.

Extract from Rupert Brooke, 'The Soldier', from Edward Marsh's Dolls' House Library book, *Georgian Poetry 1911–1921*

own books in the miniature library because they declined, such as John Masefield, or they did not respond to their invitations, such as Lascelles Abercrombie and D.H. Lawrence. Some, such as Wilfred Gibson and Fredegond Shove, do not appear to have been asked.

However, many of the poets included by Marsh did have their own books in the Dolls' House Library, including Maurice Baring, Francis Brett Young, John Drinkwater, Robert Graves, Siegfried Sassoon, J.C. Squire and James Stephens. Walter de la Mare, whose poem 'The Linnet' is in Marsh's contribution, submitted three poems to the Dolls' House on his own behalf. 'The Sleeper', 'The Listeners' and 'An Epitaph' are joined by his chilling short story, 'The Riddle'.

Some poets contributed new poems to the Dolls' House Library, or ones that had yet to be published. Aldous Huxley, most remembered now for his dystopian novel *Brave New World*, was primarily writing poetry when the Dolls' House Library was being organised, and contributed three unpublished verses that he had recently written. Having been abroad when the Princess's invitation was sent, he feared that he was responding too late, so copied 'Before Sleep Comes', 'The Mill Wheel' and 'Clouds over Carrara' into the booklet sent to him hastily. Unique poems, not found elsewhere, were also

submitted by writers who are less well known now, such as the novelist H. de Vere Stacpoole, who contributed his translations of fragments of poetry by Sappho, several of which had not previously been published, and Norman Davey, whose 'Invitation to a Wanderer' was submitted along with a pre-published poem.

A.A. Milne's offering was likewise unpublished at the time he contributed it to the Dolls' House Library. Having been Assistant Editor and a major contributor to *Punch* before the war, Milne had then had much success as a playwright. He was yet to write the *Winnie-the-Pooh* stories which would come to be so well loved, but in his newly written poem *Vespers*, which he decided to send to Princess Marie Louise and his good friend Lucas, the public first encounters the character of Christopher Robin – Milne's son.

Little boy kneels at the foot of the bed;

Droops on the little hands little gold head.

Hush! Hush! Whisper who dares!

Christopher Robin is saying his prayers.

A.A. Milne, from his Dolls' House Library book, *Vespers*

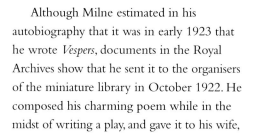

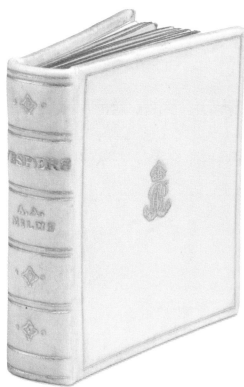

....

Left: A.A. Milne
(1882–1956)

Illustrated by E.H.
Shepard (1879–1976)

Vespers

Private Collection

Above: A.A. Milne
(1882–1956)

Vespers, 1922

RCIN 1171579

Although Milne estimated in his autobiography that it was in early 1923 that he wrote *Vespers*, documents in the Royal Archives show that he sent it to the organisers of the miniature library in October 1922. He composed his charming poem while in the midst of writing a play, and gave it to his wife,

Daphne, to do with what she wanted. Daphne had *Vespers* printed in *Vanity Fair* in 1923, and so popular and high-earning was the poem that Milne wrote that it was the most valuable present he had ever given her. He had to ask her to lend the poem back to him for inclusion in the Doll's House Library.

UNIQUE CONTRIBUTIONS

Many of the writers represented in the Dolls' House rose to the challenge set in their invitations of contributing original work. One such was G.K. Chesterton, who confirmed in a letter to Princess Marie Louise a year after he sent in his manuscript that 'it does not exist anywhere else; even in my own memory'. Chesterton, best known now for his Father Brown series of detective stories, wrote for the Dolls' House *The Ballad of Three Horns*, in which Robin Hood travels to the north of England to defeat an enormous bull, cutting off its horns and bringing them back to Friar Tuck and Little John. He had to be reminded by the Princess that he had promised to contribute, and in March 1922 sent a letter attributing his delay 'to some vague hope of doing something a little more worthy of so national & historic an object. This, I fear, it will not be in any case; but such as it is, I will certainly complete it at once.' He sent his beautifully written book just five days later.

Hilaire Belloc, Chesterton's great friend known now for his comic verse, similarly

But naught was here but the towering beast
And the ruinous falling land
When Robin lifted his soul to God
And took his bow in his hand.

There was naught alive but a living death
To freeze the stars with fear
When Robin went upon one knee
And drew the cord to his ear.

And the whole earth shook with the monster
And the whole world swayed and swam
When Robin shot, and hit the white
For the honour of Nottingham.

G.K. Chesterton, from his Dolls' House Library book,
The Ballad of Three Horns

Opposite: G.K. Chesterton (seated, left) with fellow Dolls' House contributors Hilaire Belloc (standing) and Maurice Baring
Sir Herbert James Gunn (1893–1964)
Sketch for Conversation Piece, 1932, oil on canvas
RCIN 402265

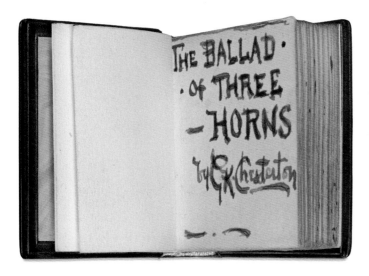

Left: G.K. Chesterton
(1874–1936)

The Ballad of Three Horns, 1922

RCIN 1171464

Below: Marie Belloc
Lowndes (1868–1947)

*Why they Married and Why
they Remained Married*, 1923

RCIN 1171443

contributed original work to the Dolls'
House Library. *Peter and Paul: A Moral Tale*
is a short story about Paul, who makes
sensible decisions, and Peter, who
makes rash, imprudent ones. Paul
achieves wealth and success, while
Peter dies penniless and alone.
Hilaire Belloc's sister Marie Belloc
Lowndes also sent in an original
piece. In *Why they Married and Why
they Remained Married*, a woman
celebrating her diamond wedding
anniversary tells the story of her
successful relationship to her young
neighbour. 'Why we remained
married? ... Why, in my young
days *everybody* remained married. I
was forty, at least, when I first had

a divorced woman pointed out to me, and
I remember how very surprised I was that
she looked just like everybody else!'

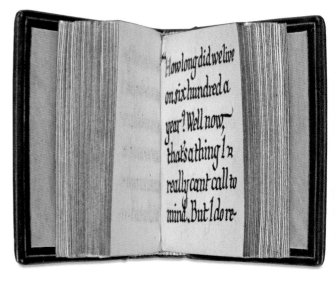

Sir Arthur Conan Doyle wrote for the Library a new, unpublished story about the famous detective Sherlock Holmes (a rare story narrated not by Watson but in the third person). In *How Watson Learned the Trick*, Watson remarks that Holmes's skills of deduction are a superficial trick that he himself can easily perform, observing that

Holmes must be expecting an important visitor because he has put on his coat, and that he has taken to financial speculation because he showed interest in the relevant page in the newspaper. Holmes cuttingly explains that he has on his coat because he is going to the dentist, and the cricket scores are printed next to the finance section.

'Anything more?'

'I have no doubt that I could find other points, Holmes, but I only give you these few, in order to show you that there are other people in the world who can be as clever as you.'

'And some not so clever,' said Holmes. 'I admit that they are few, but I am afraid, my dear Watson, that I must count you among them.'

Sir Arthur Conan Doyle, from his Dolls' House Library book, *How Watson Learned the Trick*

....

Sir Arthur Conan Doyle
(1859–1930)
How Watson Learned the Trick, 1922
RCIN 1171476

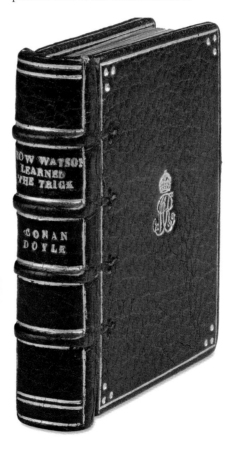

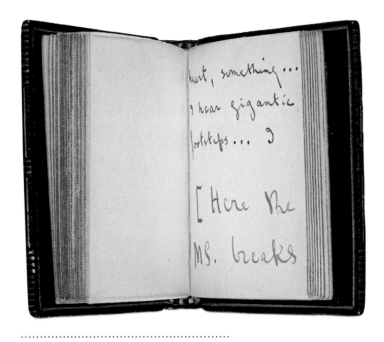
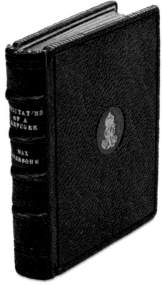

....

Above and right: Max Beerbohm (1872–1956)
Meditations of a Refugee, 1922
RCIN 1171335

Max Beerbohm, acclaimed as an essayist as well as a caricaturist, contributed an original work called *Meditations of a Refugee*. In it, the protagonist wishes to be smaller: 'By the time I was twenty-two I measured 5 feet 9¼ inches. This was not a great height, but it was immensely greater than I desired.' Unable to persuade the fairies to help him shrink, he recounts how he turned to W.B. Yeats, who looked down on him and said he was small enough already, and Sir J.M. Barrie, who 'looked up at me, said that I seemed to be unaware that I was addressing a Baronet, and disappeared in a dense cloud of tobacco smoke'. Despairing, he wills himself to be tiny, and eventually succeeds. Unable to live in the normal-sized world, he is relieved to hear of Queen Mary's Dolls' House. He breaks into it, and, hiding behind a curtain, writes his tale in one of the miniature books. Just as he begins to impart 'something worthy of this royal tome – some magical piece of prose or poetry, which a Queen would not disdain', the tale ends, with a note in different ink supposedly signed by Leslie Chaundy, Honourable Librarian of the Mansion, that the interloper was caught and ejected by the Comptroller of the Household.

Another original story was submitted by M.R. James, scholar and Provost of Eton. In August 1922 he was asked by the Princess to contribute a book to the miniature library. Famed for his ghost stories – a person who 'knows more about supernatural life than anyone living', according to E.V. Lucas in his catalogue – it was natural to suggest he wrote one called *The Haunted Dolls' House*. In the chilling tale, a wealthy collector buys a gothic dolls' house, complete with a family of dolls, and sets it up in his bedroom.

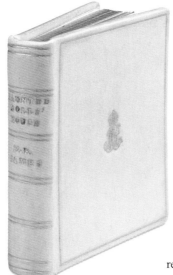

He is woken in the night by a clock chiming one, even though no real clocks are in earshot. It is from the house, which has come to life. The dolls play out a series of scenes, in which a daughter poisons her father, who then rises from his coffin to kill her children. In the morning the collector retreats to the seaside to recover, and there finds out that the story played out by the dolls was true. James's manuscript is one of the longest in the Dolls' House Library at nearly 5,000 words, but his handwriting is so small that his book is far from being the thickest.

Above left: M.R. James (1862–1936)

The Haunted Dolls' House, 1922

RCIN 1171452

Left: The telling of a ghost story depicted in the Dolls' House Library's portfolios:

Poy [Percy Hutton Fearon] (1874–1948)

Listening-In, 1922, pencil and watercolour

RCIN 927282

BEYOND BRITAIN

The Empire does not feature as strongly in the Dolls' House Library as might be expected for a British project of the 1920s. Indeed, contributions from colonies and dominions were discouraged, as an embarrassing moment revealed by the Dolls' House archive shows. Joshua Smith, a British artist then staying in Toronto, Canada, responded to his invitation to contribute a miniature drawing for the Library's portfolios with enthusiasm, deciding to paint a picture of Canada's loveliest child. This quickly got out of hand when Smith asked the *Toronto Star* to organise a nationwide competition to find the child. Amidst much national excitement, 7,640 photographs were submitted to the newspaper. The winning child, Doris Elizabeth Hyde, was duly painted and the tiny picture was provided with a platinum, diamond and pearl frame. The Editor of the *Star* asked the Canadian High Commissioner, Peter Larkin, to present it to Queen Mary as an official gift from the people of Canada. At this point E.V. Lucas heard about the endeavour, and drafted an awkward letter to the High Commissioner

The 'loveliest child', Doris Elizabeth Hyde, c.1922–3

Toronto Star Photo Archive

explaining that not only was all the wall space in the Dolls' House accounted for, but that they could not accept contributions from dominions and colonies, only individual people.

Nevertheless, there is some recognition of India. Unsurprisingly, given that it had a special status within the Empire, and that one of Sir Edwin Lutyens' other projects, running concurrently with the Dolls' House, was the design and construction of New Delhi. India was important to Queen Mary too: she felt deep attachment to it, and to Indian women in particular.

Beginning 'A Flower-offering laid at the feet of Queen Mary beloved of Her people in India, and especially of the children people and Women-people', Cornelia Sorabji's *The Flute-Player's Dolls* is the only manuscript in the Dolls' House Library to be contributed from India itself. Sorabji was the first female graduate in western India, and went on to study law at Oxford. On her return to India she dedicated herself to increasing women's access to legal representation. Her beautifully written tale is about the Hindu god Krishna capturing the spirit form of a maiden and her brothers with his flute playing, only to see them turned into egg-shaped dolls. In a postscript, Sorabji writes that these dolls are to be found at Puri, in eastern India.

Above: Lafayette Ltd

Cornelia Sorabji, 1930, whole-plate film negative

National Portrait Gallery, London

NPG X70451

Left: Cornelia Sorabji (1866–1954)

The Flute-Player's Dolls, 1922

RCIN 1171135

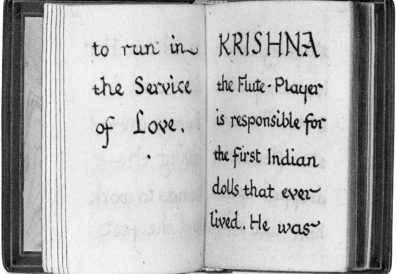

to run in the Service of Love.

KRISHNA the Flute-Player is responsible for the first Indian dolls that ever lived. He was~

Several British writers took inspiration from India, including Sir E.D. Swinton with *What the Mulberry Saw*. Swinton, who grew up in India, is credited with inventing the tank, and he usually wrote about military matters. He contributed to the Dolls' House Library under the pseudonym 'Ole Luk-Oie', a Danish term meaning 'shut-eye'. His story is about an under-ripe mulberry talking to an over-ripe mulberry, both having fallen from a tree in Kashmir. The under-ripe mulberry wonders why he fell, and the over-ripe one explains that the leopard Bagheera teased Baloo the bear, who hit the tree, shaking off the mulberry. The tale continues with Bagheera gouging Baloo's eyes leaving him half blind and covered in blood, and ends with the old mulberry dying. 'Amusing', Lutyens pronounced the book in a letter to Princess Marie Louise, 'not I fear too long'. While 'baloo' and 'bagheera' are Hindi for 'bear' and 'panther', and tales about talking animals are part of Indian oral traditions, Swinton cannot have been unaware of Rudyard Kipling's *The Jungle Book* characters.

F.W. Bain also contributed writing inspired by India. For his miniature manuscript, *Leaves of the Lotus*, he made selections from his popular love story, *A Digit of the Moon*, an invented translation of a Sanskrit manuscript, and wrote a new fable,

'A Biter Bit'. Bain is thought to have finished writing after his retirement from the Indian educational service in 1919, but for him, as for many of the contributors, the Dolls' House Library provided new impetus.

Aside from Britain and India, the only other country to have significant representation in the Dolls' House Library is Ireland. A dominion of Britain at the time, it was enjoying its great Literary Revival, and Irish artists, composers, authors and poets of both Nationalist and Unionist persuasion contributed to the Library.

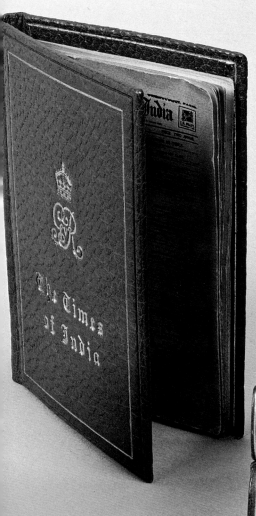

A selection of books relating to India featured in the Dolls' House Library (clockwise from left):

Sir E.D. Swinton (1868–1951)
What the Mulberry Saw, 1923
RCIN 1171514

The Times of India, 27 February 1924
RCIN 1171548

Cornelia Sorabji (1866–1954)
The Flute-Player's Dolls, 1922
RCIN 1171135

F.W. Bain (1863–1940)
Leaves of the Lotus, 1922
RCIN 1171441

....
The last page of 'In Silver'
(also known as 'Washed in
Silver')
James Stephens (1882–1950)
Poems, 1922
RCIN 1171336

....
Opposite: A selection of books by Irish
writers featured in the Dolls' House
Library (clockwise from left):

Edith Œnone Somerville
(1858–1949) and Martin Ross
[Violet Martin] (1862–1915)
*Some Extracts from the Writings of
E. Œ. Somerville and Martin Ross*, 1922
RCIN 1171417

George A. Birmingham (1865–1950)
The Curragh, 1922
RCIN 1171446

James Stephens (1882–1950)
Poems, 1922
RCIN 1171336

Lord Dunsany (1878–1957)
*Selections from 'The Chronicles of
Rodriguez'*, 1921
RCIN 1171543

Katharine Tynan (1861–1931)
Poems, 1922
RCIN 1171338

James Stephens, a committed Republican, copied nine
of his poems into the little booklet sent to him, each with
stylised illustrations, while the prolific Nationalist and
feminist writer Katharine Tynan submitted four poems.
Anglo-Irish writers represented in the Dolls' House
include Lord Dunsany, who contributed selections from
his first novel, *The Chronicles of Rodriguez* (at that point
still unpublished); and Edith Œnone Somerville, who was
famed for witty observations on the Anglo-Irish ascendancy.

Somerville copied out in bright purple ink several
passages of published work on behalf of herself and her
deceased writing partner Martin Ross, the pseudonym of
her cousin Violet Martin. Believing that there was a parallel

world of spirits, Somerville was convinced that she and Martin still wrote together. She began her miniature book with a sketch in black ink of the drunken groom Slipper, a comic character from their best-loved series *Some Experiences of an Irish R.M.*

In 1922–3 Ireland was in the throes of civil war, and the Dolls' House Library correspondence reveals the difficulties the political situation caused for its Irish contributors. When Somerville sent her completed booklet back to Princess Marie Louise in May 1922, she warned her under separate cover that she was not using

registered post, at that time, she claimed, the opposite of a safeguard. In August of that year the military painter Lady Butler (whose sister Alice Meynell compiled a miniature collection of her poems for the Dolls' House) was invited to send a watercolour for the Library's tiny portfolios. From Tipperary she replied to the Princess that, 'owing to the disturbances', she had regrettably heard nothing of the Dolls' House project, all English newspapers having been destroyed by the Republicans for the last six weeks. She would not risk sending her contribution until the country was settled.

....

Right: Letter from J.B.S.
MacIlwaine to Princess Marie
Louise, 28 August 1922

RA VIC/ADD/A/18/ML/14C/57

Opposite: Edith Œnone
Somerville (1858–1949) and
Martin Ross [Violet Martin]
(1862–1915)

*Some Extracts from the Writings
of E. Œ. Somerville and Martin
Ross*, 1922

RCIN 1171417

When the Irish artist J.B.S. MacIlwaine
wrote from County Tyrone in August 1922
in response to his invitation to contribute,
he reminded Lucas and the Princess that for
those living in Ireland the Dolls' House was a
frivolity, and contributing to it was a luxury
in which some could ill-afford to indulge:

at this moment all our time is required to
meet present needs and if possible help our
friends and neighbours who are homeless and
desolate in this country, in the circumstances,
therefore, I will contribute a work in pen and
ink 1½" x 1" before October 15th next,
upon receipt of cheque for five guineas.

Lucas's draft response shows little compassion:
'I am sorry that the scheme of the Dolls
House, which is purely voluntary, does not
enable us to accede to your request.'

'I'D RATHER PLAY WITH CHILDREN THAN COUNT THEIR GRAVES'

The First World War in the Dolls' House Library

When the Dolls' House was begun in 1921, only three years had passed since the conclusion of the First World War. Contributions to the Library reflect this: the shadow of the war as well as the desire to escape from it can be read again and again in its little manuscripts. Sir Edwin Lutyens captured this element of the project in a letter he wrote to Princess Marie Louise in November 1921. 'I hate going to France', he confided hurriedly, about to depart for one of his frequent visits to French cemeteries as part of his work with the Imperial War Graves Commission. He would prefer to be working on the Dolls' House: 'I['d] rather play with children than count their graves'.

Part of Lutyens' memorial work was designing the Cenotaph at Whitehall in London in 1919. A monument for the dead of the war and a symbol for national remembrance, it cemented Lutyens' fame. Journalist Sir Philip Gibbs, one of the best known of the British war correspondents

reporting from the battlefields of the First World War, wrote a moving account of the unveiling of the Cenotaph and the burial of the Unknown Warrior for the *Daily Chronicle*, which he adapted for his Dolls' House Library contribution.

Other offerings made in memory of the war came from John Buchan and May Bradford. Buchan, most famous now for his adventure novel *The Thirty-Nine Steps*,

> To some women...he was their boy who went missing one day and was never found till now, though their souls went searching for him through dreadful places in the night. To many men...he was a familiar figure, one of their comrades, the one they liked best, perhaps, in the old crowd who went into the fields of death...
>
> Sir Philip Gibbs, from his Dolls' House Library book, *The Unknown Warrior*

First World War books in the Dolls' House Library (from left to right):

Sir Philip Gibbs (1877–1962)
The Unknown Warrior, 1922
RCIN 1171461

May Bradford (1897–1965)
Tales from 'A Hospital Letter-Writer in France', c.1922–3
RCIN 1171419

Mary C.E. Wemyss (b. 1868)
White's Lane, 1922
RCIN 1171424

John Buchan (1875–1940)
The Battle of the Somme, 1922
RCIN 1171487

"The Silence"
J. C. Dollman, R.W.S.

The Cenotaph in the Dolls' House
Library portfolios:

John Charles Dollman (1851–1934)

The Silence, c.1922, watercolour

RCIN 926949

was too ill to see active service during
the First World War, but he worked in the
Intelligence Corps, wrote propaganda, and
published on the war prolifically. His book,
an extract from his work on the Battle of
the Somme, was tooled on both covers
by the binders Sangorski & Sutcliffe with
the phrase 'Their Name Liveth for Ever'.

Taken from Ecclesiasticus, this phrase is commonly inscribed on war memorials.

Like Princess Marie Louise, who ran a hospital for soldiers in London during the First World War, contributor May Bradford spent the war amongst the wounded. For over four years she wrote letters for British servicemen being treated in French hospitals. She published her experiences in *A Hospital Letter-Writer in France* in 1920, and made selections from this for her Dolls' House contribution. She recounted how she brought comfort by writing out the last words of dying men to send to their mothers and wives.

Perhaps the Dolls' House book which best reflects how many were feeling after the First World War is *White's Lane* by Lutyens' sister Mary, who published as Mrs George Wemyss. In this short story a woman, taken ill while nursing wounded soldiers during the war, moves to the country to convalesce. As she becomes well, she begins to walk in the nearby White's Lane. She loves the lane, and, imagining fairies living on the banks, she collects posies of wildflowers while listening to aeroplanes humming overhead and guns thudding over the sea in France. On the day she arrives at the lane to find the banks mown down, she receives a telegram with news that her son has been killed. 'All this had been hers until destruction had

come upon it, robbing it of its treasures as the war had robbed her of all that in her life was most lovely.' The story moves on two years – the war has ended, but she cannot find peace. Returning to the lane to see that the banks have regrown and the wildflowers are back, she begins to feel hope.

These are the experiences of non-combatants, but the Library features books from those who served in the First World War too, including the renowned war poets Siegfried Sassoon, Edmund Blunden and Robert Graves. Despite Sassoon writing in his diary that he agreed with the composer Sir Edward Elgar's opinion on the Dolls' House – that it is 'an insult for an artist to be asked to mix himself up in such nonsense' – he contributed his poem *Everyone Sang*, copied neatly into the little booklet he was sent. Blunden copied out the four poems he submitted, including 'Behind the Line', in which he remembers his experiences of the war, in a beautifully calligraphic hand. His artistry is complemented by his book being in one of the most stunning of the Library's bindings (see page 111).

Robert Graves mostly selected the poems for his contribution, *Poems: Abridged for Dolls and Princes*, from various of his previously published works. Short, light verses at the beginning of his book give way to darker poems. They are not about the war, but were written in an attempt to forget it, to 'escape from a painful war neurosis', as Graves later put it.

While for some contributors the Dolls' House Library was an opportunity to convey their experiences of the war and highlight the suffering and hardship it brought, for others it was, as Lutyens and Graves both expressed, a means of escaping from its horrors.

War poets in the Dolls' House Library (left to right):

Edmund Blunden (1896–1974)
Poems, c.1922
RCIN 1171435

Robert Graves (1895–1985)
Poems: Abridged for Dolls and Princes, 1922
RCIN 1171488

Siegfried Sassoon (1886–1967)
Everyone Sang, 1922
RCIN 1171480

BOOKS FOR DOLLS

Imagining the Dolls' House as a doll palace or a fairy mansion – a not altogether unreal realm of living dolls and magical creatures – also gave contributors a means of escape. Many wholeheartedly entered into the conceit that their books were to be read by doll or fairy occupants.

Originally, the organisers agreed that dolls would be included in Queen Mary's Dolls' House. Sir Edwin Lutyens and Princess Marie Louise wrote lists of the dolls they would need: notes on an early floor plan of the House, drawn by Lutyens in May 1921, list nearly 50 dolls. Along with the expected king, queen, prince and princess, with various servants, sentries and courtiers, Lutyens and Princess Marie Louise thought of including a doctor, a journalist, a Bolshevik and a suffragette. These last two suggestions were later crossed out, unsurprisingly in the case of the Bolshevik: it was Princess Marie Louise who had to break the news to her cousin the Marchioness of Milford Haven that her sister the Empress Alexandra of Russia, along with her husband and children, had been killed by the Bolsheviks in 1918.

Princess Marie Louise and Lutyens then discussed having multiple dolls for each figure represented, to save having to change their clothes.

In tiniest lines,
With the smallest pen seen,
I dedicate this
To the Dolls of the Queen....

...At midnight who knows
That they dance not nor play
Over little bright floors
Like a shadow astray?

And who can be sure
As they play by themselves
That they toy not at all
With the books on their shelves...

...And we poets are dust
Before we are read,
But the Queen's dolls I trust
To read me instead.

Lord Dunsany, extracts from the specially written dedicatory poem in his Dolls' House Library book, *Selections from 'The Chronicles of Rodriguez'*

Lutyens thought they would need nine dolls to represent the queen at different activities. He conceded this would require a large number of dolls in total but thought it would save time, as well as wear-and-tear, when arranging them into different scenes.

However, it was eventually decided that dolls would not form part of the Dolls' House. E.F. Benson, who wrote a chapter on dolls for *The Book of the Queen's Dolls' House*, explained that if the miniature rooms and objects were to be magically expanded to normal size, they might become real rooms with real, usable objects. Yet dolls, not being miniature living humans, would, if expanded, become monstrous: the illusion would be broken. The only dolls made for the Dolls' House were figures of guardsmen. As they remain so still when on duty as to be like furniture, Benson

concluded that they did not form an exception to the organisers' decision.

The lack of dolls in the House did not discourage many of the authors from being inspired to write about or for dolls, whether they were imagining them as inanimate toys or as miniature living occupants. Books about dolls include that by John Kendall, who wrote his contribution under the pseudonym 'Dum-Dum'. He submitted six poems written from a toy's point of view. One is about a doll who has been laid down on her side rather than on her back, meaning that her eyes do not shut so she cannot sleep. This doll difficulty did not prevent two writers from concluding that it is best to be a doll. A.M. Williamson, in *Doll or Fairy?*, contributed an original story about a fairy who

Miniature model guardsman made for Queen Mary's Dolls' House, *c*.1924, painted plaster
RCIN 231500

chooses to become a doll so she can live in the Dolls' House and be closer to her namesake, Queen Mary; while in Edward Knoblock's offering, a short play called *The Doll's Dilemma: A Comic Tragedy*, a doll given the option to come alive decides against it, reflecting that life will be more painful if she has a soul.

Dolls as subject matter also inspired the writer Gilbert Cannan. His contribution, *The Story of a Doll*, is told from the point of view of a doll who adores her owner, a motherless girl called Gwen. Gwen grows up, runs away from home with her doll, and marries a prince. The doll is forgotten until one day she is brought a new dress and given

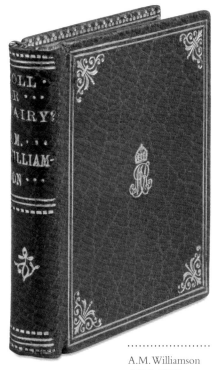

Edward Knoblock (1874–1945)

The Doll's Dilemma:
A Comic Tragedy, 1922

RCIN 1171486

A.M. Williamson
(1869–1933)

Doll or Fairy?, 1922

RCIN 1171477

Some girls treat dolls with kindness and care. Many naughty girls and dogs pull them limb from limb.... Inquisitive girls and boys wrench off the limbs to look at joints, or poke out the eyes.... Some children quarrel for the possession of a doll and pull off its head in the struggle and then howl and weep until the nurse sends the head and doll to a hospital.

Sir John Bland-Sutton, from his Dolls' House Library book, *Principles of Doll-Surgery*

to their baby. 'The Baby's name is Gwen', the doll reports, 'and at last I know a Doll's true happiness, for the new Gwen has a father and a mother and I can be a member of a real Royal Family, and no longer have thrust on me more than any Doll can bear.'

Gilbert Cannan's Dolls' House story is an illuminating insight into his thoughts during a time of personal crisis. He had separated from his wife Mary, who had previously been married to Sir J.M. Barrie, after he fell in love with a woman named Gwen. He lived with her and another man, the threesome becoming the talking point of literary London. Gwen married the other man while Cannan was on a lecturing tour

in 1920. His Dolls' House book was written in May 1922, and in the following October Gwen gave birth. Over this time Cannan became increasingly despondent. In 1924, having been unmanageably violent for some time, he was committed to asylums for the rest of his life.

One of the most interesting books about dolls in the miniature library is *Principles of Doll-Surgery* by Sir John Bland-Sutton, a famous surgeon. He outlines how injuries can be sustained by dolls, then with much technical detail he explains, with information obtained from a London dolls' hospital, how to repair them. 'No anaesthetics or antiseptics are required', his book states baldly. The writing of the book was, he informed Princess Marie Louise, a source of much amusement and pleasure.

In Bland-Sutton's book dolls are definitely inanimate objects, not living creatures, but this line is more blurred in C.H. Collins Baker's book on doll taste in art. Although it was written for a human audience, he joyfully entered into the conceit that dolls are real. An artist and art critic, Collins Baker was Keeper at the National Gallery when he contributed to the Dolls' House, and later worked for the Royal Household as Surveyor

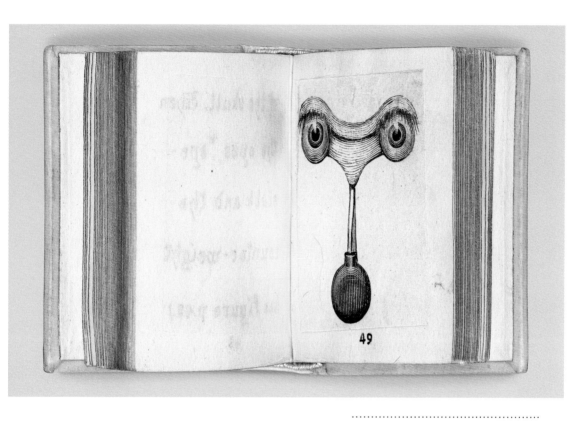

of the King's Pictures. His book is 'a little work of great erudition and much satirical mischief', as E.V. Lucas wrote in his introduction to the extract of it he printed in *The Book of the Queen's Dolls' House Library*. Collins Baker compares doll taste in art favourably to 'monster' (human) taste, all the while poking fun at art criticism, scholarship and psychoanalysis. This is one of the contributions to the Library that was specifically requested of a writer, Princess Marie Louise and

Doll eyes, eyes-stalk and counterweight. Sir John Bland-Sutton had the miniature woodblock from which this print is made produced specially in order to illustrate his Dolls' House Library book

Sir John Bland-Sutton (1855–1936) *Principles of Doll-Surgery*, 1922 RCIN 1171413

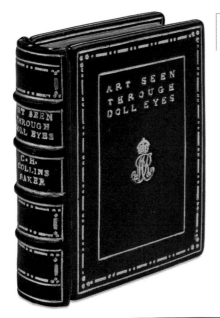

So thorough is the art culture of the educated class in Doll land that as a matter of course a reasonable knowledge of Art history and practice is regarded as part of the education of a gentleman. This, of course is a very different outlook from ours. For we expect our educated class to 'know nothing, you know, about Art, but only what I like.' And we don't even understand that what we like is generally bad.

C.H. Collins Baker, from his Dolls' House Library book, *Art Seen through Doll Eyes*

Above and right:
C.H. Collins Baker
(1880–1959)

Art Seen through Doll Eyes, 1922

RCIN 1171420

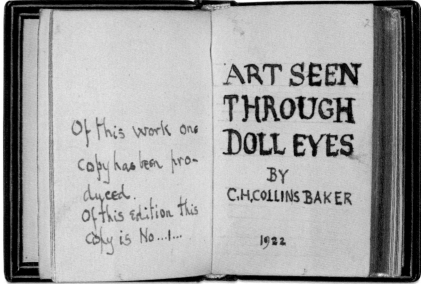

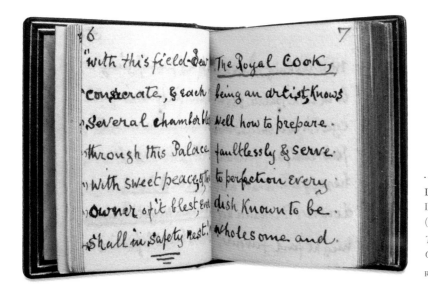

6

7

"with this field-dew
consecrate, & each
several chamber this
through this Palace
with sweet peace the
owner of it blest; and
shall in safety rest!

The Royal Cook,
being an artist knows
well how to prepare.
faultlessly & serve.
to perfection every
dish known to be.
wholesome and.

Left and below:
Dame Agnes Jekyll
(1861–1937)

*The Doll's-House
Cookery-Book, c.*1922

RCIN 1171529

Lucas having written to Collins Baker to suggest
that a little manual dealing with art would be
very acceptable.

Dame Agnes Jekyll, a well-known society
hostess who wrote a series of articles on
housekeeping and domestic management, also
blurred the line with reality in *The Doll's-House
Cookery-Book* she wrote for the miniature
library. She eschewed her friend Lutyens' initial
suggestion (as he recounted in a scrawled letter
to Princess Marie Louise) to write 'take a
sparrows egg & keep it stirring with a feather
of Tom Tit', instead giving the quantities
required in recipes for human consumption,
'trusting to the kitchen weights and measures
in the Dolls' House to weigh all things in due

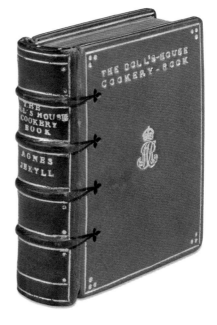

95

E.V. Lucas
(1868–1938)

*The Whole Duty
of Dolls*, 1922

RCIN 1171559

A popular sweet from Scandinavia called *Röd-Grö*, or Rothe Grütze.

Boil currants and raspberries with a little water and sugar in the proportion of two pounds of fruit to a tea-cup of water and a ¼ lb. white sugar. Pass through a sieve; put into an enamel stewpan with a large teaspoon of sieved arrowroot, stirring gently but continuously till smooth, and of a gooseberry fool consistency. Serve very cold with fresh cream and plain dry boiled rice in cut glass dishes.

Dame Agnes Jekyll, 'Röd-Grö, or Rothe Grütze', from her Dolls' House Library book, *The Doll's-House Cookery-Book*

proportion and to scale' for the dolls. Her recipes include breakfast brioches, *Consommé à l'Indienne* (a curry of chicken or rabbit which she describes as a comforting soup for dinner) and a Danish red fruit pudding called *Röd-Grö*.

A number of the Dolls' House books were written specifically for dolls to read. Lucas's contribution, the smallest of the handwritten books submitted, was *The Whole Duty of Dolls*: a collection of maxims, or moral guidance, based on *The Whole Duty of Man*, a popular devotional book first published in the seventeenth century. 'It is the

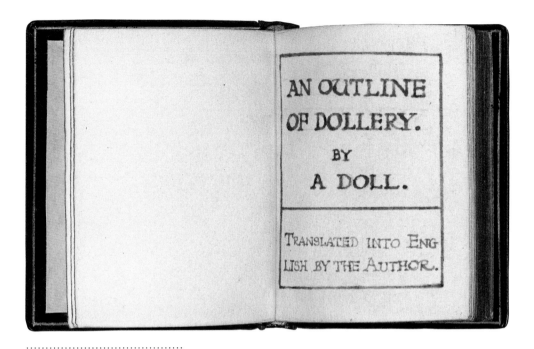

Sir E. Denison Ross (1871–1940)

An Outline of Dollery, by a Doll, 1923

RCIN 1171524

whole duty of dolls to comfort their owners. It is their privilege, too. This is done mainly by perfect placidity and silence', Lucas advises. Viscount Esher, a courtier who, together with fellow Library contributors A.C. Benson and G.E. Buckle, had edited volumes of Queen Victoria's letters, also wrote maxims with a thought to a doll audience: 'Every Doll has her day' and 'Love me, love my Doll' are written alongside more general words of advice including 'Every healthy man should make ten mistakes a day' and 'Avoid the hardened frivolist'.

Being an ideal home for a doll king and queen, the Dolls' House contains books that would be of use to its diminutive occupants. Manuscript reference works include a history of dolls by Sir E. Denison Ross, essential to any doll library. Lutyens had initially suggested to Denison Ross, the first Director of the School of Oriental and African Studies, that he contribute a poem in Arabic, but Lucas, thinking of

THE QUEEN'S DOLLS' HOUSE

CATALOGUE OF WATER COLOUR & OTHER DRAWINGS AND ETCHINGS

WINDSOR CASTLE 1924

Frederick Muller (active 1923–4)

The Queen's Dolls' House: catalogue of watercolour & other drawings and etchings, 1924

RCIN 1171522

The theatre critic A.B. Walkley was told by Lucas and the Princess that it would be very amusing if he contributed a work of dramatic criticism for dolls. His *Histrionics for Dolls: A Letter to a Debutante* is advice to a doll who wishes to become an actress. Her permanently painted red cheeks, Walkley writes, will serve her well when encountering dialogue that has escaped the censor, while her inability to hold anything will save her from being troubled with bouquets at the end of her performance. Walkley is rather unkind when comparing the doll to real actresses: 'they will appear stiff and wooden; you will be truly so'. Lutyens, annoyed that Walkley was considering publishing his *Histrionics for Dolls* before the Dolls' House was completed, wrote unreasonably in a letter to the Princess that he considered the book to be 'a rather silly story'.

Books were provided in the Dolls' House Library to enable the supposed doll household to carry out the running of the House. These include a tiny manuscript stud book for the

the difficulties of printing Arabic in his planned anthology, intervened to suggest that it would be more amusing to write something in English. Denison Ross's offering, *An Outline of Dollery, by a Doll*, is a history and anthropology of dolls, written for dolls, complete with spurious footnotes. Chapter III begins, 'The early history of our race is still shrouded in mystery, but we have every reason to believe that the first man created had children, and that those children insisted on having dolls.'

horses and a handwritten catalogue of the contents of the Library's art portfolios, which lists alphabetically the artists who contributed. Francis Berry, of Berry Bros. & Co., wine merchants to the Royal Family, compiled a list of the contents of the Cellar, with instructions on how best to store and serve the wine. The small bottles in the Cellar still contain real wine, champagne and whisky.

The blurring of the line between reality and fantasy when writing for the Dolls' House is what gives the miniature library much of its charm.

W. & A. Gilbey [London]
Crate of Chateau Laudenne wine,
*c.*1922–4, wood and green glass
RCIN 231120

Left: Francis Berry (active 1922)
Stock of Wines and Spirits in the Cellars of the Royal Dolls' House at Windsor Castle, 1922
RCIN 1171511

99

FAIRIES

The Dolls' House being a somewhat enchanting home, it is not surprising that several of the contributors to its Library were inspired to write about fairies, elves and similar magical beings. Fairies and folklore were popular themes for poets and authors of the late nineteenth and early twentieth centuries: they provided a means of escape from modernity into a sentimentalised, ideal past.

Fairies appear in poems selected for the Dolls' House by Alfred Noyes, Rudyard Kipling and Robert Bridges. Kipling included his poem 'The Fairies' Siege' in his miniature collection, whilst amongst the poems contributed by Alfred Noyes, best known now for his poem 'The Highwayman', is one called 'The Elfin Artist' from a collection he had published in 1920. Like many of the participants, Noyes was no stranger to writing about fairies, having written the introduction to an anthology of fairy poetry in 1908.

Given that the Dolls' House was conceived of as an ideal royal residence in miniature, it is natural that Oberon and Titania, king and queen of the fairies in William Shakespeare's *A Midsummer Night's Dream*, would be drawn on for several of its Library's books. Sidney Colvin, as well as contributing extracts from his friend Robert Louis Stevenson's works, copied out 'The Song of Titania' from Shakespeare's play; Agnes Jekyll quotes Oberon in the preface to her book on cookery; and Sir Frederick Pollock, a dignified law historian, wrote *Queen Titania's Chancellor*, an original short tale about Titania and Oberon seeking a judge for their palace. Titania designs a wig for their judge, sized so that its wearer must have wisdom, valour, justice and mercy in ideal proportion. Fairy messengers, searching

In a glade of an elfin forest
When Sussex was Eden-new,
I came on an elvish painter
And watched as his picture grew.
A hare-bell nodded beside him.
He dipt his brush in its dew.

Alfred Noyes, first stanza of 'The Elfin Artist', from his Dolls' House Library book, *The Elfin Artist*

From the Dolls'
House Library's
portfolios:

MacDonald Gill
(1884–1947)

*The Fairies' Dolls
House, c.*1922,
pen and ink and
watercolour

RCIN 927023

Sir Frederick Pollock (1845–1937)

Queen Titania's Chancellor, c.1923

RCIN 1171525

for one who might fit such a wig, cannot find anyone perfect enough. Dolls' House Library contributor Lucy Clifford, having discussed with Pollock his book, wrote to Princess Marie Louise that she thought he was more pleased with his Dolls' House story than with any of his big professional achievements.

Edith Wharton also contributed an original work. In her poem, *Elves' Library*, she claims fairy origins for the Dolls' House Library: two young elves, bored on a rainy day, created a library for their mother. The poem describes how the elves consult a carpenter bird to make the shelves and a bookworm to advise on how books are made. Their mother, reading of the Dolls' House project in a copy of *The Times*, determines her library will form part of the 'Ideal Home we'd all so gladly live in'.

> ... While, in walnut ink,
> A lady-Spider wrote impassioned
> Novels – only think!
>
> Edith Wharton, from her Dolls' House Library book, *Elves' Library*

The Dolls' House Library's 'most remarkable possession', as E. V. Lucas describes it in his catalogue of the books, is an illustrated fairy tale. It is by C. Kenneth Bird, the cartoonist known as 'Fougasse' – a name he took from the word for a First World War mine.

Left: Howard Coster (1885–1959)

A Portrait of Fougasse (C. Kenneth Bird), 1937

Mary Evans Picture Library, Peter & Dawn Cope Collection

Below: From a set signed for Queen Mary by Fougasse in 1940

Fougasse (1887–1965)

Careless Talk Costs Lives: '… Strictly Between These Four Walls', c.1940, colour lithograph

RCIN 1194573.e

Like Lucas, Fougasse was a contributor to *Punch*. He would go on to become Editor and to design the Second World War 'Careless Talk Costs Lives' series of posters for which he is still remembered today. Queen Elizabeth II, when Princess Elizabeth, commented in 1950 'how carelessly we should have talked during the war but for Fougasse'.

Fougasse contributed *J. Smith*, a tale of a fairy who is blown out of Fairyland during a storm, and falls into Eaton Square in London. He pretends to be human to see how well his fairy talents, considered mediocre in Fairyland, will be received. He tries dancing, then music, then art, all to great public acclaim, but his performances and his painting are derided by jealous professionals. Disheartened, he returns to Fairyland where he is joyfully welcomed home. Beautifully illustrated in Fougasse's distinctive, brightly

"…. strictly between these four walls!"

CARELESS TALK COSTS LIVES

....

Fougasse (1887–1965)

J. Smith, 1922

RCIN 1171321

coloured style, with the pictures and text skilfully combined, the book is indeed one of the treasures of the miniature library.

Fairies were not merely a figment of the imagination at this time: some of the Dolls' House contributors genuinely believed that they were real. In 1920 and 1922 Sir Arthur Conan Doyle, who wrote the Sherlock Holmes stories including an original one for the Dolls' House, published photographs of fairies taken by two girls, Frances Griffiths and Elsie Wright, in Cottingley, near Bradford. He believed that these proved the existence of fairies. The photographs also convinced fellow Dolls' House contributor H. de Vere Stacpoole, but in fact the girls had faked them by using cardboard cut-outs of illustrations from *Princess Mary's Gift Book*, a collection of children's stories published in 1914. Griffiths and Wright found that they could not admit to faking the photographs without making Doyle look like a fool, and it was not until 1983 that they confessed.

*Frances and Leaping
Fairy*, August 1920

Science & Society
Picture Library

CHILDHOOD

Although dolls' houses are usually thought of as children's toys, the overwhelming majority of the books submitted to Queen Mary's Dolls' House Library, even those about dolls and fairies, were for adult readers. Authors who primarily wrote for children were not asked for contributions. However, when the novelist Max Pemberton wrote to Princess Marie Louise to ask if the content of his little book should be for dolls, adults, or a fairy story for children, the Princess replied suggesting he write a fairy story. His little book, *Lion Heart*, in which a boy conquers mountains while leaving the fairies and the flowers behind, is a fable about growing up bravely, helping others and accepting life's challenges.

While the journalist Filson Young dedicated his little book 'to the children of the house', his essay is more suitable for older readers, it being an erudite *Philosophy of Toys*. Other writers to contribute works for children were Fougasse, who repeatedly referred to his illustrated manuscript as a 'children's book' in his letters to Princess Marie Louise even though his story's message about the jealousy of professional rivals is better understood by adults, and the author

M. E. Gray.

From the Dolls' House Library's portfolios:
Millicent Etheldreda Gray (1873–1957)
Mary Had a Little Lamb, *c.*1922, watercolour
RCIN 927039

and playwright W. Somerset Maugham, who penned a children's fairy tale. *The Princess & the Nightingale* is about a young princess named September, sweet and charming in comparison with her bitter sisters. She finds companionship with a talking nightingale, and, not wanting to lose him, she keeps him in a cage. When he no longer sings and refuses to eat she realises that because she loves him she must set him free. This story was also not exclusively for children, however, as its later publication in a literary magazine shows.

W. Somerset Maugham (1874–1965)

The Princess & the Nightingale, 1922

RCIN 1171526

It appears the Dolls' House was supposed to be reminiscent of the childhood experienced by the adults of the 1920s, rather than be a plaything for the younger generation. F. Tennyson Jesse, a writer whose great-uncle was the poet Alfred, Lord Tennyson, lovingly invokes the imagined fantasy town of her childhood in

My Town, but asks of it 'do you figure at all in the minds of children brought up to the clear hard certainties of to-day, when Pilots have succeeded Pirates, and wireless taken the place of wizards?'.

In his philosophical contribution, Filson Young wrote that he believed an extremely elaborate model such as the Dolls' House would be too complete to satisfy a child's imagination. Instead, as the intended audience of the majority of the books shows, the House was an escape from reality for adults, albeit with its playful nature undermined by the more serious intent to record the 1920s for posterity.

'Let me out, let me out.'

'Don't be such an old silly,' said September. 'I've only put you in the cage because I'm so fond of you. I know what's good for you much better than you do yourself. Sing me a little song and I'll give you a piece of brown sugar.'

But the little bird stood in the corner of his cage, looking out at the blue sky, and never sang a note. He never sang all day.

W. Somerset Maugham, from his Dolls' House Library book, *The Princess & the Nightingale*

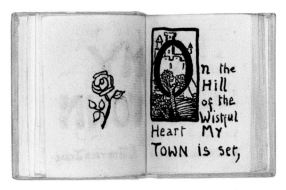

F. Tennyson Jesse (1888–1958)

My Town, 1922

RCIN 1171550

AUTOGRAPH BOOKS

It was not only literature that Princess Marie Louise and E. V. Lucas wanted to represent in the Dolls' House Library's manuscripts. They organised four miniature autograph books for significant people from the Army, the Navy, Parliament and the Theatre to sign.

Earl Haig, the Field Marshal in command of British troops during the First World War, was approached first for the Army's book, now sadly lost. 'Be so good as to let me know what names should fill it', Lucas wrote in his draft letter to Haig, 'beginning of course with your own'. One hundred pages long, it was bound by the prominent bindery Sangorski & Sutcliffe along with the other autograph books and sent round to eminent officers of the Army from May 1922.

The autograph book of the Navy contains 97 signatures and is headed by John Jellicoe, who was First Sea Lord from 1916 to 1917. At the time of the book's circulation

Autograph book of the Navy, c.1922–4

RCIN 1171053

he was Governor-General of New Zealand, which might explain why his signature seems to have been a late addition, squeezed on to the back of the silk flyleaf at the front of the book. This makes the signature on the first proper page, that of Earl Beatty, First Sea Lord at the time, the second in the book. Perhaps there was some competition between the two as to whose name would be first: there was much controversy over their conflicting accounts of the 1916 Battle of Jutland.

The first name in the book signed by politicians, known as the autograph book of statesmen, is that of Arthur Balfour, 1st Earl of Balfour, who had been Prime Minister from 1902 to 1905. In total there are 40 signatures in this book, including those of seven prime ministers, past

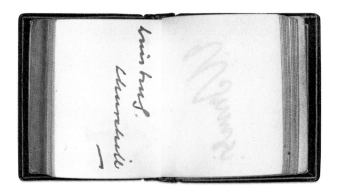

Left: Signature of Winston Churchill (1874–1965) in the autograph book of statesmen, c.1922–4

RCIN 1171052

Below: George Frederic Watts (1817–1904) *Ellen Terry ('Choosing')*, 1864, oil on strawboard

National Portrait Gallery, London

NPG 5048

(Balfour and H.H. Asquith), present (David Lloyd George and Bonar Law, who were both Prime Minister in 1922) and future (Stanley Baldwin, Neville Chamberlain and Winston Churchill).

Ellen Terry, the now elderly but still adored actress, headed the names recorded in the autograph book of the stage, while her less-famous sister Marion Terry signed towards the end. In all, 67 stars of the London theatre signed the book, including Marie Tempest, Violet Vanbrugh, her sister Irene, and Irene's husband Dion Boucicault the younger. Many of the signatories, like Matheson Lang and Sir Johnston Forbes-Robertson, were also screen actors working at a time when 'talkies', films with sound, were the latest innovation. One of the most famous British film stars of the time, Charlie Chaplin, did not sign. It might have been hoped that he would: in September 1921 he visited

Sir Edwin Lutyens in his offices and was thrilled to see the Dolls' House being built. He also promised to send in a miniature self-portrait, but appears not to have found the time.

'THE LITTLE BOOKS LOOK DIVINE'

Binding the Dolls' House Library

· · · · · · · · · ·

SOPHIE KELLY

THE BOOKS THAT ADORN THE SHELVES of the Dolls' House Library are remarkable not only for their contents; the leather bindings that cover each of the 176 miniature manuscripts constitute one of the greatest collections of twentieth-century fine bindings in the United Kingdom. These jewel-like bindings, each finely decorated in gold with exquisite designs, are the work of some of the most prestigious binderies of the 1920s. The four workshops that were asked to contribute to the Library demonstrated extraordinary skill and expertise in their commissions, and their bindings were highly praised by the Dolls' House organisers. 'The little books', Sir Edwin Lutyens wrote to Princess Marie Louise after seeing some of the finished, fully bound books for the first time, 'look divine'.

Though the early decades of the 1900s saw a boom in designer bookbindings, the 1929 Wall Street Crash and the depression that followed had a lasting impact on the trade, causing many of the major firms, including those involved in the Dolls' House Library, significantly to reduce their staff and output, or even to close. The decline of the fine binding industry after 1929 makes the Dolls' House collection all the more significant: as one of the last major

·····································
Opposite: Edmund Blunden (1896–1974)
Bound by Sangorski & Sutcliffe
Poems, c.1922
RCIN 1171435

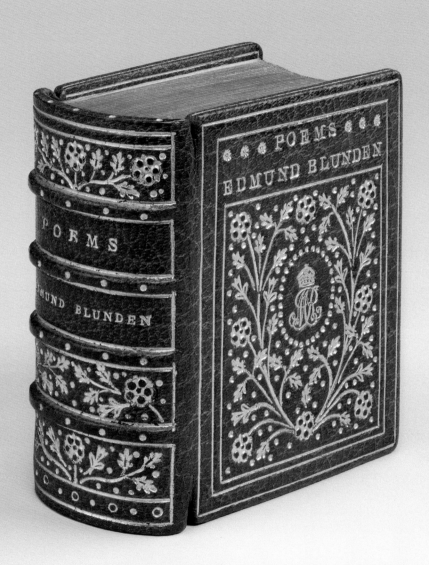

commissions of this period, the bindings were, and remain, an outstanding showcase of one of the golden ages of bookbinding.

From the very earliest stages in the planning of the Dolls' House Library, the question of how the miniature books should be bound formed an important part of the organisers' considerations. Before authors had even been asked to compose their manuscripts, Lutyens approached the firm Riviere & Son, a well-established bindery that had been producing fine bindings since the 1820s, to enquire about the possibility of having these little books bound. Stuart Riviere Calkin, the firm's owner, advised Lutyens that 75 miniature books would cost £50 to bind (just over £2,000 in today's money). The expense, Lutyens justified in a letter to the Princess, was surely worth it, 'for the labour & time spent in binding miniature books is immense'. Despite this cost, Riviere offered to bind 25 of the Dolls' House books free of charge.

Anticipating that the Dolls' House Library would require the binding of considerably more than 25 books, the organisers enlisted three more prestigious binderies to undertake this delicate task. Two of these workshops, Birdsall & Son and Zaehnsdorf, had been producing fine bindings since the early nineteenth century. The Zaehnsdorf bindery was particularly

renowned, having bound books for Queen Victoria, King Edward VII, King George V and Queen Mary.

Established in 1901 by expert bookbinders Francis Sangorski and George Sutcliffe, Sangorski & Sutcliffe was by far the newest of the binderies asked to contribute to the Dolls' House. By the 1920s, their sumptuously bound volumes had come to rival those by the well-established firms. In their first year of business they bound books for King Edward VII; the following year, with Zaehnsdorf and Riviere as competitors, they won the contract to bind the Westminster Abbey service books for his Coronation. The firm became celebrated for their elaborate 'jewelled bindings', which were adorned with gold leaf, jewels and other precious materials such as pearl.

Sangorski & Sutcliffe initially promised to bind ten books for the Dolls' House free of charge. George Sutcliffe was particularly enthusiastic about the opportunity of producing these miniature bindings, writing to E. V. Lucas that he would like to keep binding beyond the ten they had offered 'until [the Dolls' House] is properly furnished with a Library of bound books'. He ended the letter by boldly suggesting: 'I wish unless the post is already occupied to be the bookbinder for the Library.' With other binderies enlisted, this was unfortunately not a role Lucas was

Finishers' department,
Sangorski & Sutcliffe
workshop, *c*.1920

Sangorski & Sutcliffe
Archive

able to grant Sutcliffe. George Sutcliffe was undeterred. 'I would not wish', he noted in a letter to Princess Marie Louise, 'to deprive any of my colleagues of the joy of sharing with me the binding of one of the most wonderful libraries in the world'.

Whilst not quite earning the title of 'bookbinders for the Dolls' House Library', Sangorski & Sutcliffe contributed more bindings than any of the other firms: in total, 135 of the miniature books were bound in their workshop. Riviere also went above and beyond the 25 they had initially offered, binding 19 manuscripts and 45 printed books. Zaehnsdorf and Birdsall were slightly more reserved, contributing nine

and six bindings respectively. A small handful of books, often those that were submitted slightly late, were bound elsewhere in smaller, lesser-known binding workshops.

Though the process of binding the miniature Dolls' House books would have been largely the same as for any normal-size volume, the four binderies had to make some adjustments to account for the smallness of their task. The leather used to bind the books, for example, needed to be incredibly thin to allow the little booklets to open, but not so thin that the binding would snap. Achieving this delicate balance was the responsibility of the bindery's forwarding department, who would pare, or scrape,

....

Matt Stockl, Conservator
Bookbinder in the Royal Bindery,
Windsor Castle, gold-tooling a
miniature book, 2019

the leather to the required thinness before covering each book.

Once covered, the little bound books were then sent to the finishing department, each to be decorated with their own individual design. The bindings are all decorated using a process called gold tooling. To achieve this, a finisher first coats the leather in glair (beaten and strained egg white) over the areas to be decorated, before applying thin sheets of gold leaf. A brass tool engraved with a specific design such as a flower or swirl is then heated and pressed over the gold, sealing it into the leather; the excess gold leaf is wiped away, leaving behind a pattern in the shape of the tool. The process of gold tooling on the miniature Dolls' House books required particular skill, as the brass tool could easily be pressed too firmly on to the book and break through the thin leather. None of the Dolls' House books bound by the four major firms shows any signs of this occurring; the gold tooling is in fact so pristine and delicate as to suggest the finishers that worked on them were the most accomplished of their day.

The Dolls' House organisers decided that the miniature library should be bound according to a genre-specific colour scheme. Novels were to be covered in red leather, poems in light blue and essays in green. To ensure each book was bound in the correct colour, certain binderies were sent specific subjects. Sangorski & Sutcliffe, for example, were the only bindery to be sent the poetry manuscripts, the majority of which they bound in beautiful light blue-grey leather. Novels, which comprised over 50 of the manuscripts made for the Dolls' House, were sent to Sangorski & Sutcliffe, Birdsall and Riviere. Zaehnsdorf were sent only essays and articles, all of which they bound in dark green leather. A good number of the tiny manuscripts made for the Library inevitably fell outside the categories of novels, poetry or essays, and were bound in a variety of coloured leathers.

With the bindings being completed across multiple workshops and in different coloured leathers, something was needed to ensure that all the miniature books could be identified as belonging to the Dolls' House Library. In a practice that dates back to at least the sixteenth century, finely bound books are often stamped in the centre with the arms, heraldry or monogram (intertwined initials) of the library or owner to which they belong. Just like their larger counterparts, it was decided that the Dolls' House books should be stamped with the monogram of their owners. Though the Library had initially been conceived as a room for the king, it soon evolved into a space also designed to be used and occupied by a queen, due in a large part to the involvement of Queen Mary herself. In the early stages of the planning of the Library bindings, however, the organisers seemed to have considered having the books stamped only with the arms or initials of King George V. Princess Marie Louise wrote to John Fortescue, the Royal

'MR' monogram on
Oscar Browning (1837–1923)
Bound by Sangorski & Sutcliffe
Edelweiss, 1922
RCIN 1171473

Librarian, with the idea that the model for the Dolls' House monogram could be based on those stamped on books for the Royal Library. In his reply, Fortescue explained that he had 'no settled rule as to stamping books for the Royal Library … sometimes we stamp with the Royal arms, sometimes with G. R., sometimes with a monogram; sometimes with plain G; sometimes with GG; sometimes with a crown alone without any letters'. The making of miniature tools to stamp on the books would also, he noted, 'take a little time & cost a little money – not a great sum, but in these days one has to look to shillings & such pence – so at least I find in the Library'.

The Dolls' House organisers evidently thought this was a price worth paying. George Sutcliffe was asked to organise the production of identical tiny brass monogram tools, and to distribute these among the other major binderies. The design eventually decided upon, the intertwined initials MR for *Maria Regina* (Queen Mary) beneath a crown, recognised Queen Mary's increasing role in the Library's formation.

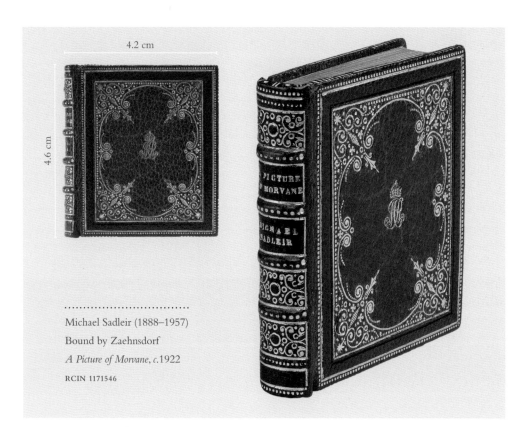

4.2 cm

4.6 cm

Michael Sadleir (1888–1957)

Bound by Zaehnsdorf

A Picture of Morvane, c.1922

RCIN 1171546

Once bound in coloured leather, nearly every book in the Dolls' House was gold-tooled in the centre of the front cover with this miniature monogram.

Aside from the 'MR' monogram supplied to them and some direction as to the colour of leather to use, the workshops involved in the binding were allowed a fair amount of freedom as to the design and decoration of the miniature books. In a letter to George Sutcliffe, Princess Marie Louise made this quite clear: though the 12 books of poetry she was sending to him 'are to be bound in light blue', the 'tooling & design are left to you'.

Each of the binderies decorated the Dolls' House books sent to them in styles typical of their workshops. Zaehnsdorf were known for their elaborately gold-tooled but fairly traditional, nineteenth-century designs, and their Dolls' House bindings are all in this fashion, with formal, gold-tooled borders and swirling vines in each of the corners. *A Picture of Morvane* by Michael Sadleir is perhaps Zaehnsdorf's finest: numerous vines, swirls, stars, flowers and *pointilles* (small dots) are exquisitely arranged in a looping circle around the 'MR' monogram. The books bound by Birdsall are also decorated with distinctly 'Victorian'-style designs, with delicate dotted borders and floral tools on the inside corners.

Riviere perhaps showed the most variation in the types of bindings they produced for the Dolls' House. Like Zaehnsdorf and Birdsall, some of their designs are reminiscent of nineteenth-century bindings, with swirling floral borders and spines profusely decorated

Bindings by Birdsall & Son
(left to right):

Archibald Marshall (1866–1934)
The Twins & Miss Bird, 1922
RCIN 1171422

Max Pemberton (1863–1950)
Lion Heart, 1922
RCIN 1171415

George A. Birmingham (1865–1950)
The Curragh, 1922
RCIN 1171446

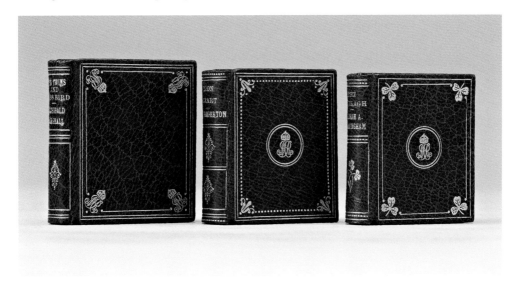

Geometric bindings by Riviere & Son
(left to right):

Frank Swinnerton (1884–1982)
The Boys, 1922
RCIN 1171406

Frank Frankfort Moore (1855–1931)
The Way to Keep Him, c.1922
RCIN 1171432

Eden Phillpotts (1862–1960)
The River Dart, c.1922
RCIN 1171400

with leaves, vines and flowers. Others, such as the binding for *The Way to Keep Him* by Frank Frankfort Moore, with its intertwining rope-like border, and Eden Phillpotts' *The River Dart*, with its simple but elegant interlocking diamond and square, reflect a much more modern, twentieth-century approach to design. Perhaps the most impressive of this group is the binding for *The Boys* by Frank Swinnerton, which is gold-tooled on both covers with a twisting geometric design of intertwined diamonds and looping squares. This type of pattern would have been completed with pallets, brass tools with straight lines of varying lengths that could be used together to 'build up' a design of continuous lines. To execute a looping design without overrunning one pallet line through another would be difficult on an average-sized volume; to achieve this on a miniature book is even more remarkable.

Another bindery to embrace twentieth-century design in its approach to the Dolls' House bindings was Sangorski & Sutcliffe. Like Riviere, several of their contributions draw on geometric motifs emerging in the wider design world of the early twentieth century. Joseph Conrad's *The Nursery of the Craft* or Maurice Baring's *Elegy on the Death of Juliet's Owl*, for example, both incorporate multiple square and rectangular borders with circular motifs of dots and circles in each of the corners. The binding for Charles L. Graves' *Norfolk* is also tooled with particularly fine interlacing, geometric borders. One of the most striking of the Sangorski & Sutcliffe contributions is the gold-and-black chequered decoration on the wonderful mustard-yellow binding for *The Chronicles of Rodriguez* by Lord Dunsany. These motifs all find parallels in the Art Nouveau movement of the late nineteenth and early twentieth century, which similarly championed flowing lines and organic, geometric shapes.

Geometric bindings by Sangorski & Sutcliffe (left to right):

Charles L. Graves (1856–1944)
Norfolk, 1922
RCIN 1171554

Lord Dunsany (1878–1957)
Selections from 'The Chronicles of Rodriguez', 1921
RCIN 1171543

Maurice Baring (1874–1945)
Elegy on the Death of Juliet's Owl, 1922
RCIN 1171475

Joseph Conrad (1857–1924)
The Nursery of the Craft, 1922
RCIN 1171555

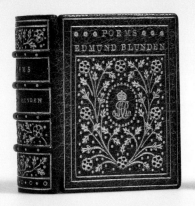

Flower bindings by Sangorski & Sutcliffe
(left to right):

Edmund Blunden (1896–1974)
*Poems, c.*1922
RCIN 1171435

A.S.M. Hutchinson (1879–1971)
From 'If Winter Comes', 1922
RCIN 1171456

Edward Marsh (1872–1953)
Georgian Poetry 1911–1921, 1922
RCIN 1171412

Another feature typical of the Sangorski &
Sutcliffe bindery is their use of rich floral decoration.
These flower-filled designs are often so densely
applied to the bindings that they almost completely
obscure the leather. The blue-grey volume for
Edmund Blunden's *Poems*, for example, is beautifully
decorated all over with leafy vines and round flowers,
their five petals picked out with tiny pieces of red
leather. *If Winter Comes* by A.S.M. Hutchinson is even
more highly decorated, this time with holly leaves,
red berries and sprouting white flowers. Another
sumptuous floral binding was chosen for the book
on Georgian poetry, which is tooled in the centre
with a large open-work four-petal flower around the
monogram, with sprouting flowers and leafy vines in
each of the four corners.

In many of their designs for the tiny bindings,
Sangorski & Sutcliffe paid close attention to the
book's content. A typical example of this approach
is the binding for Oscar Browning's poem *Edelweiss*,
decorated on both covers and spine with minute white

flowers the colour and shape of the edelweiss flower. Another is Oliver St John Gogarty's collection of poems entitled *Apples of Gold*, tooled with a border of hanging golden apples. Some bindings were even designed with the authors themselves in mind: the collection of poems by the Irish author Katharine Tynan and the little volume with extracts from Somerville and Ross's books about Ireland were both tooled in the corners with shamrocks (see page 81).

Some books appear to have been designed in thematic groups. Several works related to Christmas, including Arnold Bennett's *Christmas Eve and New Year's Eve*, *A Merry Xmas* by Victor Bridges, as well as *If Winter Comes*, are all bound in red and decorated in gold with the same holly leaf and berry tools. The night sky is also a recurring theme, with books related to stars or the night, such as Sir Julian S. Corbett's *Slumber Songs* or H. de Vere Stacpoole's edition of Sappho's poetry,

Above: Oscar Browning (1837–1923)
Bound by Sangorski & Sutcliffe
Edelweiss, 1922
RCIN 1171473

Right: Oliver St John Gogarty
(1878–1957)
Bound by Sangorski & Sutcliffe
*Apples of Gold, c.*1922
RCIN 1171442

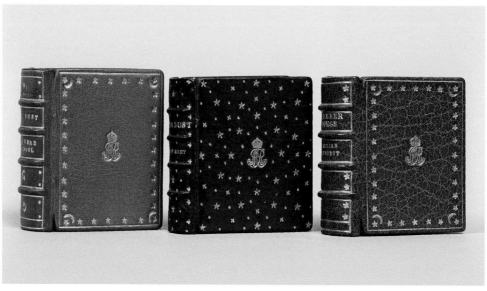

Themed bindings by Sangorski
& Sutcliffe

Opposite (above from left to right):
Victor Bridges (1878–1972)
A Merry Xmas, 1922
RCIN 1171450

A.S.M. Hutchinson (1879–1971)
From 'If Winter Comes', 1922
RCIN 1171456

Arnold Bennett (1867–1931)
Christmas Eve and New Year's Eve, 1922
RCIN 1171401

Opposite (below from left to right):
H. de Vere Stacpoole (1863–1951)
Star Dust, or Verses from Sappho, 1922
RCIN 1171474

Pamela Grey (1871–1928)
*Star Dust, c.*1922
RCIN 1171491

Sir Julian S. Corbett (1854–1922)
Slumber Songs, 1922
RCIN 1171333

Star Dust, gold-tooled with a border of stars and crescent moons. A beautiful example of this motif is also used on the identically titled *Star Dust* by Pamela Grey, though this time the deep-blue leather is gold-tooled all over with tiny stars, reflecting a clustered night sky.

Each of the autograph books is decorated to reflect the occupations of their signatories (see page 108). The book for the Navy, for example, is tooled with an anchor in each corner of the strapwork border, whilst the book for statesmen, or politicians, is bound in brown and tooled with simple gold and black fillet lines in a very formal, statesman-like design. The book for stage actors is the most accomplished of the group, showing a classical stage decorated with tiny actors' masks above and below a hanging curtain.

Autograph book of
the stage, *c.*1922–4

Bound by Sangorski
& Sutcliffe

RCIN 1171054

An example of a 'historic' binding
by Sangorski & Sutcliffe:

G.K. Chesterton (1874–1936)

The Ballad of Three Horns, 1922

RCIN 1171464

F. Anstey (1856–1934)

Bound by Sangorski & Sutcliffe

The Wisdom of Piljosh, 1922

RCIN 1171448

shown next to one of the
Royal Library's finest examples
of a medieval binding

Flavius Josephus (37–after 93)

*Josephi historiog[ra]phi viri clarissimi
prologus* (Augsburg: Johann
Schussler, 1470)

RCIN 1055413

Sangorski & Sutcliffe's other method of reflecting
something of the content of the book was to bind the
miniature volumes with a 'historic' or 'religious' theme in
an intentionally antiquated fashion. Books such as G.K.
Chesterton's *The Ballad of Three Horns*, a poem about Robin
Hood, or *The Reading of the Bible* by J.G. Frazer, are bound in
a rich brown leather and tooled with a simple design similar
to medieval-style bindings. The most impressive of these
'historic' bindings was made for F. Anstey's *The Wisdom of
Piljosh*. This large, chunky binding is blind-tooled (decorated
without gold) with a 'panel' design, so called because it
was typically executed with one brass block or panel. The
binding also has raised corners, into which small metal studs

Fougasse (1887–1965)

Bound by Sangorski & Sutcliffe

J. Smith, 1922

RCIN 1171321

have been pressed, another feature found on medieval bindings. These 'old-style' bindings reveal Sangorski & Sutcliffe's knowledge of and sensitivity to historic binding techniques.

Perhaps the most remarkable of the Sangorski & Sutcliffe content-themed bindings is their sumptuously gold-tooled and painted white-vellum binding for the contribution by cartoonist 'Fougasse' (C. Kenneth Bird). Fougasse's little story about a fairy that accidentally arrives in London is beautifully illustrated throughout by the cartoonist's characteristic energetic line drawings. The fairies, depicted with round little bodies and yellow flapping wings, are also painted on both covers and the spine. This wonderful painted binding is testament to the care taken by the Sangorski & Sutcliffe bindery to design bindings that fully reflected the text and content of the Dolls' House books.

With their sumptuous leathers, delicate gold tooling and intricate, well-thought-through designs, the bookbindings are one of the most remarkable aspects of the entire Dolls' House project. The care and attention that each of the workshops paid to the binding of these tiny books resulted in a unique and intimate miniature library on a scale that had never before been realised.

In bringing together four of the leading British binderies of the early twentieth century, the organisers of the Dolls' House Library built an impressive collection that encapsulated one of the greatest eras in binding history. As one of the last major commissions of this period, the 176 finely bound manuscripts present a unique and unparalleled record of the skill and talent of bookbinders in the 1920s. Though small, this beautiful and sumptuously bound group of miniature books far outshines collections of twentieth-century fine bindings in other, human-sized libraries.

PRINTED
BOOKS

· · · · · · · · · ·

THERE ARE 132 ITEMS IN THE Dolls' House
Library which are printed books, newspapers
or magazines. Many were published before the
1920s when the miniature house was being
organised, and were gifts sent in by donors,
approved by Sir Edwin Lutyens to ensure they
were of the correct scale. However, a significant
few of the printed items were commissioned
specially for the project. They were selected
with a view to what an ideal library should
contain, and what the supposed Dolls' House
Library users – a doll king and queen and
their household – would find most useful.

The oldest book in the Library is *Biblia*,
a miniature abbreviated Bible made for
children in 1727. Producing scaled-down
versions of the Bible was popular: it being
easily portable meant it could be consulted
at will. There are ten Bibles or extracts of

the Bible in the Dolls' House, all kept in the
Library apart from a New Testament, kept in
the Princess Royal's Bedroom.

Texts of other religions are included in
the Dolls' House. There is a Qur'an, printed
by David Bryce of Glasgow in around 1900.
Bryce was a prolific publisher of miniature
books, which he produced by photographing
down existing, normal-sized books, and he is
well represented in the Dolls' House Library.
His Qur'ans, like his Bibles and dictionaries,
were usually sold enclosed in a metal locket,
which had a magnifying glass set into it. They
were carried as talismans by Muslim soldiers

· ·

Opposite: *Biblia* (London: R. Wilkin, 1727)
RCIN 1171272

A selection of almanacs from
Queen Mary's Dolls' House
(below, from left to right):

L'Ami de la jeunesse 1819
(Paris: Le Fuel, 1819)

RCIN 1171583

Le Tableau de la vie: année 1821
(Paris, 1820)

RCIN 1171103

*London Almanack for the Year of
Our Lord 1733* (London:
Company of Stationers, 1732)

RCIN 1171279

Letitia Elizabeth Landon (1802–38)
*Schloss's English Bijou Almanac
for 1839* (London: Schloss, 1838)

RCIN 1171099

Almanach auf das Jahr 1818
(Karlsruhe: C.F. Müller, 1817)

RCIN 1171341

fighting with Allied troops in the First World War. The
Library's Pentateuch, or the first five books of the Bible,
printed in Hebrew in the late nineteenth century, would
also have been supplied in a metal locket.

There is a good selection of miniature almanacs in
the Dolls' House, which can be found in the Queen's
Bedroom and Sitting Room as well as in the Library. Tiny
almanacs were first produced to provide handy useful
information such as a calendar, exchange rates and details
of high tides, but they soon developed into decorative
objects containing illustrations and poems, often given as
gifts. The oldest almanac in the Dolls' House is the *London
Almanack for the Year of Our Lord 1733*, while perhaps the
most beautiful is *Almanach auf das Jahr 1818*, a rare copy of
a German almanac encased
in a jewel-like cover.

As well as these treasures,
the Dolls' House Library
boasts a copy of what was
for a long time the smallest
book to be printed in
English using tiny metal

type, rather than more modern photographic methods. It is called *The Mite*, and it was printed in Grimsby by Ernest A. Robinson in 1891. Less than two centimetres high, it contains an odd selection of information such as 'First Paper Mill opened in England, 1588' and '150 different colours are now obtained from coal tar'. Robinson presented a copy for the Dolls' House in 1921.

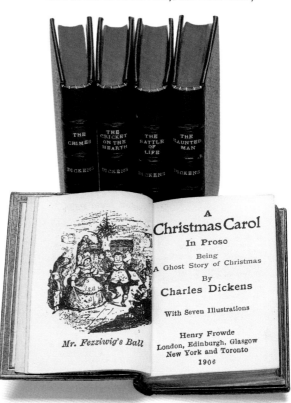

The Mite (Grimsby: E.A. Robinson, 1891)

RCIN 1171100

The printed books in the Dolls' House are not all reference works. Literature is represented by a 40-volume set of the complete works of William Shakespeare, published by David Bryce in 1904. Edited by J. Talfourd Blair, the series is dedicated to the famous actress Ellen Terry, and each clearly

Books by Charles Dickens (1812–70):

A Christmas Carol
(London: Henry Frowde, 1906)
RCIN 1171065

The Chimes (London: Henry Frowde, 1906)
RCIN 1171062

The Cricket on the Hearth
(London: Henry Frowde, 1904)
RCIN 1171063

The Battle of Life
(London: Henry Frowde, 1906)
RCIN 1171064

The Haunted Man and the Ghost's Bargain
(London: Henry Frowde, 1906)
RCIN 1171066

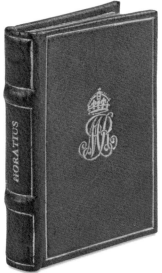

printed volume has an illustration next to the title page. Similarly produced is a five-volume set of Charles Dickens' Christmas stories. Both sets have been uniformly bound by the bookbinding firm Riviere.

To complete the Library, the organisers asked printers and publishers of normal-sized books to submit specially printed miniature versions. The finest of these was printed by C.H. St John and Cicely Hornby at their private press, the Ashendene Press, in 1923. On first being asked by Princess Marie Louise and E.V. Lucas to present the Dolls' House with a little book, C.H. St John Hornby refused, explaining that he could not find small enough metal type from which to print. However, he later realised that he could photograph down a book he had already printed, and chose *Carmina sapphica*, poems by the classical Roman poet Horace. The Hornbys produced around ten further miniature copies as gifts for family. The first of these to be bound was placed in a press overnight as part of the usual binding process, but when the binder came to collect it in the morning he found that it had been crushed into a pulp, so delicate and fragile was the volume.

Left: Horace
(65–8 BC)

Carmina sapphica
(London: Ashendene Press, 1923)

RCIN 1171318

Below: *Stanford's Atlas of the British Empire* (London: Edward Stanford, *c.*1922–3)

RCIN 1171556

Other miniature printed books supplied to the Dolls' House at the request of Princess Marie Louise and Lucas were *Who's Who*, with biographical information for significant people living in 1922, and *Whitaker's Almanac* for 1923. Both were specially miniaturised to a twelfth of full size by their publishers, as were the *ABC Alphabetical Railway Guide* and a 1923 copy of *Bradshaw's General Railway and Steam Navigation Guide for Great Britain and Ireland*, should the doll king and queen wish to plan a journey.

In a letter to the Princess, George Sutcliffe of the bookbinding firm Sangorski & Sutcliffe wrote that, as Lutyens had his heart set on a miniature atlas for the Dolls' House Library, he would source one for him from the publishers Edward Stanford Ltd. The atlas, with 12 double-page maps, was, Edward Stanford believed, the smallest ever produced. The publishers later printed copies for general sale, based on the Dolls' House original.

Copies of popular magazines such as *Country Life*, edited by Lutyens' good friend Edward Hudson, and an edition of *The Architectural Review*, which contains a tiny article about the Dolls' House itself, were photographed down and miniaturised for the library collection, as were newspapers including *The Times* and *The Morning Post*. These periodicals can be found throughout the House, not just in the Library, providing easy and informative reading material for the supposed occupants, including the servants: the short-story magazine *The Strand* is in the Housekeeper's Room, while the Linen Room has a copy of the fashion magazine *Weldon's Ladies' Journal*.

This collection of miniaturised printed items invaluable to any tiny domestic realm was completed when Lord Edward Grosvenor donated perhaps the most important one of all: an insurance policy for the contents of the Dolls' House, with cover provided by the Aviation & General Insurance Company. This indispensable document was kept in the Library's miniature safe.

The collection of printed material in the Dolls' House Library contains rare examples of miniature printing along with specially and uniquely commissioned miniaturised publications. Although in danger of being overshadowed by the manuscripts, it is an extremely significant collection of miniature printed works in its own right.

Below: *Miniature History of England* (London: Goode Bros, *c.*1901)

RCIN 1171048

Opposite: Aviation & General's insurance policy for Queen Mary's Dolls' House, 20 December 1922

RCIN 1171568

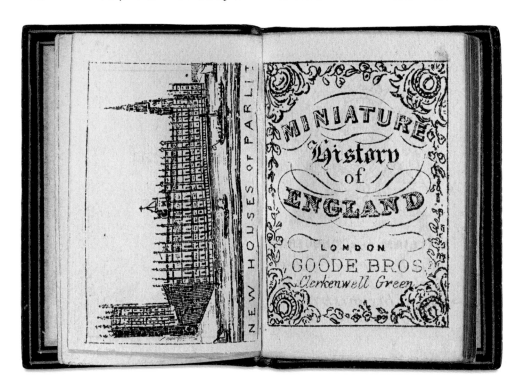

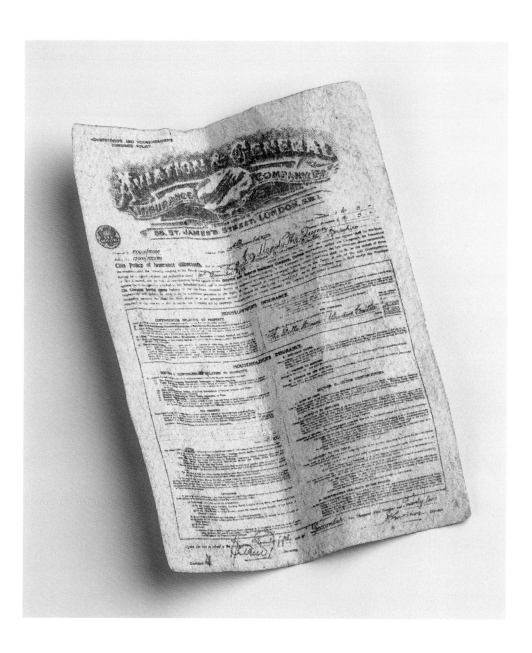

'ONE OF ROYALTY'S FAVOURITE OCCUPATIONS'

Music in the Dolls' House

· · · · · · · · · · ·

EMMA STUART

No HOUSE OF THIS STYLE AND period would have been complete without music. To lack the means to make or listen to music in a dolls' house designed to reflect great houses of the period would have been completely inaccurate. As the musicologist Edward Dent wrote in *The Book of the Queen's Dolls' House* in 1924, music was 'one of royalty's favourite occupations'. The Royal Family's own establishments were well stocked with musical instruments, sheet music and gramophones, the sheet music and gramophone records traditionally being the responsibility of the Royal Library. The Dolls' House was no different.

Princess Marie Louise moved easily through cultured society of the 1920s, mixing with artists, writers and musicians of the day. In this milieu it is likely that she became acquainted with the composer Adela Maddison (1862–1929), who had been a part of the musical life of London high society from the 1880s. She is known for introducing many of Gabriel Fauré's works to a British audience; in turn he gave her lessons in composition. In 1915 Maddison received permission to dedicate her setting of the Longfellow poem 'The Building of the Ship' to King George V. Perhaps this was the catalyst that drew her to the Princess's attention.

Maddison became active in compiling the musical content of the Dolls' House

Opposite: Page from *The Sketch*, vol. 72, 16 November 1910, featuring a portrait of Adela Maddison

Illustrated London News Ltd, Mary Evans Picture Library

COMPOSER OF THE NEW OPERA, "THE TALISMAN."

Another Triumph for Ireland !

MRS. ADELA MADDISON, WHOSE NEW OPERA, "THE TALISMAN," IS TO BE GIVEN AT LEIPZIG
ON SATURDAY (19TH).

It is expected that the production of the opera "The Talisman," which is the work of an Irish composer, Mrs. Adela Maddison, will be the event of the musical
season at Leipzig. Dr. Hans Loewenfeld, Director of the Opera House, was so delighted with the score when the composer played her work to him a few months
ago that he accepted it on the spot. The mounting is to be on a most elaborate scale, and the thirteenth-century Italian dresses have been specially designed by
Professor Steiner-Prag, of the Royal Academy of Art of Leipzig. Mrs. Maddison is supervising the rehearsals, but Herr Egon Pollak will conduct. So great is
Dr. Loewenfeld's confidence in "The Talisman" that he has already provisionally entered it for eight performances.—[*Photograph by E. Schneider.*]

....

Above and below: Adela Maddison
(1862–1929), *Vierter Aufzug*
(London: Novello & Co., 1922)

RCIN 1171280

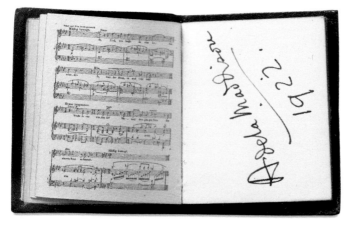

Library, creating a representative selection of the works of leading living composers. Unlike the main commissioned Library collection, which was compiled chiefly from manuscripts, the collection of music scores was put together from printed works, photographed and reduced by the publishers Novello's, and bound in purple or royal blue bindings, with the crown and the royal cypher stamped on the front cover. They were each signed and dated by their composers, except for that of Sir Hubert Parry, whose work was included posthumously.

Of the composers selected, some are still well known. Frederick Delius, Gustav Holst and Arnold Bax are familiar names, and most people could sing something by Parry, even if they did not know that he had written 'Jerusalem'. *Solemn Melody* by Sir H. Walford Davies is still played at the Cenotaph each Remembrance Sunday, while Edward German's sub-Gilbert and Sullivan operetta *Merrie England* is revived periodically in English opera houses.

The composers who provided music for the Dolls' House were for the most part (16 out of 25 contributors) connected with the Royal College and Royal Academy of Music, past pupils or colleagues of Sir Charles Villiers Stanford, who was himself a contributor. They formed a tight-knit circle of musicians.

George Bernard Shaw summed up the general situation in typically ironical style:

If you doubt that [Stanford's oratorio] Eden *is a masterpiece, ask Dr Parry and Dr Mackenzie, and they will applaud it to the skies. Surely Dr Mackenzie's opinion is conclusive; for is he not the composer of* Veni Creator, *guaranteed as excellent music by Professor Stanford and Dr Parry? You want to know who Parry is? Why, the composer of* Blest Pair of Sirens, *as to the merits of which you only have to consult Dr Mackenzie and Professor Stanford.*

Needless to say, Sir Alexander Mackenzie, as well as Parry, was a contributor! Mackenzie was considered the finest Scottish composer of his day, while Parry, his reputation and popularity enhanced by his music for Queen Victoria's Golden Jubilee celebrations in 1887, became President of the Royal College of Music in 1895. As a supporter of women's suffrage, Parry also had connections with the only woman composer other than Adela Maddison to be represented in the Dolls' House – Dame Ethel Smyth, a suffragette, friend of Emmeline Pankhurst and composer of the song 'The March of the Women', the anthem of the women's suffrage movement.

Annotated by Dame Ethel Smyth, and presented by her to Queen Mary in 1934
Dame Ethel Smyth (1858–1944)
Illustrated by Margaret Morris (1891–1980)
The March of the Women
(London: The Woman's Press; London: Breitkopf and Härtel, 1911)
printed music score with colour lithograph cover
RCIN 751071

Smyth had the distinction of being the only composer also to contribute a manuscript book to the Dolls' House Library.

Parry, Stanford and Mackenzie were leaders of the so-called English musical renaissance of the late nineteenth and early twentieth centuries, centred at the Royal College. English composers were considered to have broken away from continental influences and begun writing in a distinctive manner. Several of the Dolls' House group other than the triumvirate above were identified as being chief proponents of the renaissance: Arthur Bliss, Frank Bridge, Gustav Holst and John Ireland.

In contrast with this, other contributors – Roger Quilter, Frederic Austin, Arnold Bax and Eugene Goossens – were associated with what was known as the Frankfurt Group: musicians who had studied composition under Iwan Knorr at the Hoch Conservatory in Frankfurt in the late 1890s. They were characterised by their resistance to the English musical renaissance and the conservatism of the English musical establishment in general.

Some composers were no doubt selected for their obvious royal connections. Sir Frederick Bridge was the organist at Westminster Abbey from 1875. He directed the music at several royal events, including Queen Victoria's Golden Jubilee in 1887, and both the coronation (1902) and funeral (1910)

of King Edward VII. He had been a protégé of George Elvey, organist at St George's Chapel at Windsor Castle, and became a member of the Royal Victorian Order (an order granted by the Sovereign for personal service to the Royal Family). Elvey also linked contributors Sir H. Walford Davies and Sir Hubert Parry, and he was succeeded as St George's organist by another contributor, Sir Walter Parratt.

Other participants were drawn into the Dolls' House group, despite existing outside such networks. One such was Delius. Born in Yorkshire to German parents, he lived in Germany and France for most of his life, but still wrote works that encapsulated a quintessential Englishness, such as 'On Hearing the First Cuckoo in Spring', written in 1912. Another, Lord Berners, was an aristocratic eccentric who delighted in painting moustaches on his family portraits; he was musically self-taught, composing as a hobby, but in a quite distinctive style. Adela Maddison herself, despite her society connections and her leading role as music librarian and curator for the Dolls' House, came from outside the usual British musical establishment, her work being far better known in mainland Europe than in her country of birth.

Some of the omissions from the group of composers contributing to the Dolls' House Library are as surprising (to a modern audience) as the inclusions. Where was Sir Edward Elgar in this collection, or Ralph Vaughan Williams? The omission of Vaughan Williams is particularly surprising given his modern reputation: he played a key role in the English Pastoral School (known by its detractors as the Cow Pat School), and his work, heavily influenced by Tudor music, was crucial in the English folk-song revival. His credentials at the time were also strong: he was an alumnus of the Royal College of Music, where he had been a pupil of both Parry and Stanford, and he was a close friend of Holst.

There is at least no doubt as to why Elgar was not included – he was asked, and refused. Siegfried Sassoon recorded in his diary of 1922 Elgar's diatribe on the request:

> We all know that the King and Queen are incapable of appreciating anything artistic; they have never asked for the full score of my Second Symphony to be added to the Library at Windsor. But as the crown of my career I'm asked to contribute to a Doll's House for the Queen! I've been a monkey-on-a-stick for you people long enough. Now I'm getting off the stick. I wrote and said that I hoped they wouldn't have the impertinence to press the matter on me any further. I consider it an insult for an artist to be asked to mix himself up in such nonsense.

The group of composers assembled by Adela Maddison contributed a variety of music, chiefly vocal, with a few instrumental pieces. Several of these are dance pieces, such as *Highland Dances* by J.B. McEwen, Parry's *Gigue* or Edgar Bainton's *Country Dance*. More sober was Walford Davies' contribution *Solemn Melody*. A few of the works were specifically intended for children, appropriate for the Dolls' House if not composed deliberately for it: *The Hardy Tin Soldier* by York Bowen, based upon a Hans Christian Andersen story, Stanford's *The Broken Toy* and *The New Toy*, from his suite of six pieces for children, and *Fairy Lullaby* by Roger Quilter. But the majority of the music pieces were intended for the adult dwellers in the House. They are most often works set to poetry, such as Tennyson's *Crossing the Bar* (set by Sir Frederick Bridge), Kingsley's *The Knight's Leap* (set by Parratt), Keats's *Adoration* (set by Frank Bridge) and Robert Graves' *The Lady Visitor in the Pauper Ward* (set by Berners).

A library of sheet music also requires something to play it on. The inhabitants of the Dolls' House were provided with two instruments: an upright 'cottage' piano for the children in the Nursery, and a grand

....

Cecil J. Sharp (1859–1924)

Nursery Songs from the Appalachian Mountains
(London: Novello & Co., *c.*1921)

RCIN 1171158

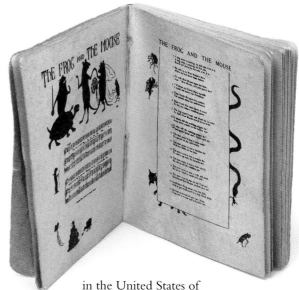

piano, painted by the watercolour artist
Thomas Matthews Rooke in the style
of the Pre-Raphaelite artist Sir Edward
Burne-Jones, for the adults in the Saloon.
Both pianos were supplied by John
Broadwood & Sons, Royal Warrant
holders and suppliers of pianos to
kings since George II. The grand piano
was designed by Dolls' House architect
Sir Edwin Lutyens, who had previously
designed pianos, including one in a case of
panelled oak which won gold at the 1900
Exposition Universelle in Paris. The dolls'
grand piano is a nine-inch gilded wonder,
painted inside and out with mythological
scenes. Like all other apparatus in the House,
it works perfectly, so long as you have a pin
to hand to strike the ivory and ebony keys.

The upright for the Nursery was
deliberately more compact and came with
its own small supply of miniature printed
music suitable for children, such as *Nursery
Songs from the Appalachian Mountains*,
collected by Cecil J. Sharp. Chief architect
of the English folk-song revival, he had
spent much of the First World War travelling

in the United States of
America lecturing and collecting
folk songs; the Appalachians provided a
feast of surviving folk songs, which had been
protected by the very remoteness of the area.

If the doll children got bored with
piano music, refused to practise or simply
showed no aptitude, they could also turn to
the gramophone for entertainment. (It had
been placed in the Nursery rather than in
any more prominent place at the behest of
Queen Mary, who confided to Princess Marie
Louise in September 1922 that 'G. [the King]
hates them!'.) This had been supplied by Alfred
Clark, Managing Director of the Gramophone
Company, who in October 1922 wrote to
Lutyens to offer a miniature functioning
gramophone in order to make the Dolls'
House more exactly like a modern home.

With the machine he offered minuscule records: 'These records will reproduce quite well, and I had in mind having some of the leading singers make them, as I feel sure they would be only too delighted to do for such an object.' This mirrors his efforts in Paris in 1907, where he set up the Musée de la Voix to preserve for posterity the voices of great singers in the archives of the National Opera House, Paris (an initiative for which he was granted the Légion d'Honneur). No such luck in this instance: the only records that are housed in the Dolls' House play (predictably enough) the National Anthem!

Gramophone Co.,

Miniature gramophone, 1922, mahogany

RCIN 230220

John Broadwood & Sons

Designed by Sir Edwin Lutyens (1869–1944); painted by Thomas Matthews Rooke (1842–1942)

Miniature concert grand piano, c.1921–4, painted wood and gilt metal

RCIN 230960

'I SHALL BE PLEASED TO ADD MY ATOM OF ART'

Prints and Drawings in the Dolls' House Library

· · · · · · · · · ·

KATE HEARD

WHEN THE WOLVERHAMPTON PAINTER and printmaker John Fullwood wrote to thank Princess Marie Louise for her invitation to contribute a drawing to the Library of the Dolls' House, he noted that 'The idea is, I think, quaint & pretty, & I shall be pleased to add my atom of art.' One of the works on paper presented to the Dolls' House by nearly 650 artists who answered the invitation to take part, Fullwood's 'atom' is a skilful watercolour, showing two children sailing a boat on a river in a golden dusk. Like many of his colleagues, Fullwood rose to the challenge of the Dolls' House commission, happy to contribute to a project which was intended both as a gift for Queen Mary and to form a collection of the best art of the time.

By 1922, Fullwood was representative of an earlier generation whose technical care and bucolic subjects persisted in the British watercolour tradition. He was not the oldest artist to contribute to the project: that distinction appears to have lain with the 92-year-old Benjamin Williams Leader, who supplied a pencil landscape drawn in a shaking yet determined hand. The youngest artist was probably Clarke Hutton, born in 1898. The elderly Leader and the youthful Hutton represent the chronological extremes of 643 artists from across the British Isles who produced works especially for the project. In total, this small army contributed 774 works on paper to be placed in cabinets in the Library. These contemporary commissions were joined by two miniature wash drawings by Clarkson Stanfield and two prints by Samuel Henry Baker, produced before the Dolls' House

John Fullwood, R.B.A., F.S.A.

John Fullwood (1854–1931)

Autumn Afterglow, Shepperton-on-Thames, c.1922, watercolour

RCIN 927005

B. W. Leader, R.A.

Benjamin Williams Leader (1831–1923)

*Trees, c.*1922, pencil

RCIN 927139

was conceived, but added to the Library collection on account of their size.

By the spring of 1922, it had been decided that a collection of watercolours, prints and drawings would be placed in portfolios in cabinets, and Princess Marie Louise began the vast task of writing personally to individual artists to invite them to contribute. Works to be included, her letter specified, should be 1½ by 1 inch (3.8 × 2.5 cm), and could be in pen and ink, pencil, watercolour or etching. These were to be submitted loose, and after submission would be placed in uniform mounts 2½ by 1½ inches (6.4 × 3.8 cm) to fit portfolios of the same size. Each mount was lettered with the artist's name and professional affiliations on the front. Titles were recorded on the backs, which sometimes also included inscriptions by the artists themselves. It is thus we learn that *The Glamour of Kashmir*, a luminous watercolour by Herbert Alexander, was 'painted without bodycolour', and that Nellie M. Hepburn Edmunds' portrait *Eileen* showed 'a favourite model'.

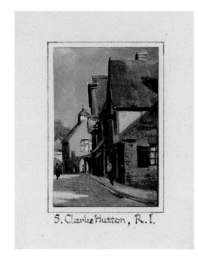

5. Clarke Hutton, R.I.

Clarke Hutton (1898–1984)

*Old Houses in a Street, c.*1922, bodycolour

RCIN 927101

The project represented, as it was intended to, the range of British achievement in the

Clarkson Stanfield , R.A.
1793 - 1867.

Clarkson Stanfield (1793–1867)

Fonthill Abbey, *c.*1820, pencil and wash

RCIN 927400

House portfolios. Practically, too, watercolour and etching could be worked successfully at such a small scale: Alice Squire noted in her letter accepting the invitation to contribute that 'water-colours are a medium favourable for delicate work & minute detail'.

Princess Marie Louise wrote in her autobiography that the Dolls' House project was conceived to 'enable future generations to see how a King and Queen of England lived in the twentieth century, and what authors, artists, and craftsmen of note there were during their reign', and the artists approached to contribute drawings and watercolours were undoubtedly those seen as representatives of the best in their field. There is no

field of works on paper, and particularly in the techniques of watercolour and etching, in which British artists were considered especially skilled. The art of watercolour had been honed in the eighteenth century by artists such as Paul Sandby, and carried to new technical brilliance in the nineteenth century by figures such as J.M.W. Turner and John Ruskin. An international revival of the art of etching, begun in the late nineteenth century and persisting into the twentieth, had inspired a generation of important British practitioners, among them Frederick Landseer Maur Griggs and Stanley Anderson, both of whom contributed to the Dolls'

Nellie M. Hepburn
Edmunds (d.1953)

Eileen, A Favourite Model,
1922, watercolour on ivory

RCIN 926962

145

evidence for the way in which the selection was made, but many of those included were members of professional societies such as the Royal Society of Miniature Painters, Sculptors and Engravers, the Royal Society of British Artists, the Royal Watercolour Society and the Royal Society of Painter-Printmakers. Although many members of these societies were approached, it is clear that invitations were not sent to all: when Marcella Claudia Heber Smith submitted an unsolicited drawing, she noted that she was 'a member of the Royal Society of British Artists and of the Women Artists and for several years an exhibitor at the Royal Academy'. None of these memberships had

yet guaranteed her an invitation, but her watercolour of yachts was gladly accepted and included in the library collection.

Beyond the professional societies, artists were chosen on the basis of word-of-mouth recommendation. A much-annotated list held amongst the Dolls' House papers in the Royal Archives gives a fascinating insight into the ways in which possible artists were identified. It is written (in an unidentified hand) on headed notepaper from Small Downs House in Sandwich, the home of Frederick Leverton Harris, a retired politician and amateur artist, and seems to have been based on a conversation with Harris. It includes a list of artists,

Frederick Landseer Maur Griggs (1876–1938)

An Old Bridge, c.1922, pencil and wash

RCIN 927043

Marcella Claudia Heber Smith (1887–1963)

Yachts, 1922, watercolour

RCIN 927380

Mark Gertler (1891–1939)
Head of a Woman, *c*.1922, pencil
RCIN 927019

Mark Gertler.

some of whom had recently mounted
'one man shows'. Some of these were
certainly approached, since works by Mark
Gertler and Edgar Rowley Smart, both of
whom are listed, appear in the collection.
Rowley Smart, it was noted, was 'a friend of
A[ugustus] John' and 'best in watercolour', a
verdict borne out by the elegant, technically
skilled work which he submitted. Included
in the list are a number of members of the
'Bloomsbury Group' – Roger Fry, Duncan
Grant and Vanessa Bell – who, if they were
invited to contribute, failed to do so, as is the
case with Wyndham Lewis (also on the list), a
superb draughtsman and founder member of
the strikingly modern Vorticist movement. If
the collection was intended to represent the
best in British art, it seems there were certain
of the best who did not wish to be included.

Another draft list of artists 'to be prodded
& given 4 weeks' provides the names of a
handful of more traditionally Establishment
figures who did not contribute. Among these
were Sir John Lavery (who had promised
'to paint small ascot pictures for portfolios'
but failed to deliver, although he did provide

E. Rowley Smart.

Edgar Rowley Smart (1887–1934)
Landscape, *c*.1922, watercolour
RCIN 927375

a pair of portraits of King Edward VII and Queen Alexandra for hanging in the Dolls' House Saloon) and Muirhead Bone. The 'prodding' did produce one result: a pencil sketch of the interior of St Mark's, Venice, by Frank O. Salisbury, a favourite portraitist of high society.

If some had no interest in participating, others, much like some of the contributing book authors, were defeated by the challenges

Frank O. Salisbury (1874–1962)

*The Vestibule of St Mark's, Venice, c.*1922, pencil

RCIN 927343

of the miniature format. The problem was summed up by Alfred Munnings (another who failed to contribute), who noted tersely in a letter to Princess Marie Louise: 'It will be a case of a very sharp point on the pencil.' Bernard Ottewell was one of a number of artists who wrote to explain that 'failing eyesight & trembling limbs do not aid one in doing the drawing the size of a postage stamp'. Some of those who struggled to work to the tiny scale must have felt, with the 82-year-old Philip Harry Newman, that 'difficulty in seeing such miniature drawing may rob me of a very great privilege'. Happily, Newman's fears proved unfounded, and he was able to submit three works which showed his skill in applying not only watercolour but also gold paint. Others were unable to complete the task. On 25 May 1923, Charles Ricketts wrote to explain that 'I cannot say with what regret I have found it impossible to work on the fairy scale required for the Doll's House; I have felt like the Camel striving to enter the eye of the needle. I can only beg you to pardon my failure & lack of graciousness which I ascribe to eye sight & age.' A day later, Ricketts' partner Charles Haslewood Shannon also threw in the towel, writing that he had 'reluctantly been obliged to give up hope of doing a drawing for the Dolls House.

Philip Harry Newman
(1840–1927)

The Annunciation, c.1922,
watercolour, ink and
gold paint

RCIN 927225

I am aware how stilted and stupid this will
seem to you & must beg you to overlook
this failure in which eyesight and a hand
no longer used to delicate linework have
conspired to make me useless.'

Those artists who did contribute works
approached their commissions in myriad
ways. For some, the Dolls' House setting
was a key factor, and prompted depictions
of children and fairy-tale subjects.
Others considered the royal nature of the
commission, and produced portraits of
members of the Royal Family or depictions
of royal residences. Many artists offered

Harold Arthur Burke (1852–1942)

Windsor Castle, c.1922, watercolour

RCIN 926867

Elisabeth Brockbank, R.M.S.

G. E. Studdy.

George E. Studdy (1878–1948)

A Laughing Dog, c.1922, pencil and watercolour

RCIN 927412

Elisabeth Brockbank (1882–1949)

The Old Quaker Lady, c.1922, watercolour

RCIN 926847

topographical depictions, with subjects ranging from the British Isles to the Middle East. Numerous portraits were submitted, some of identified sitters (among them the Duke of Northumberland, and the nine-month-old 'Lorna of Bath'), others of unnamed figures such as the *Old Campaigner* painted by William Wainwright and the *Old Quaker Lady* who was the subject of a watercolour by Elisabeth Brockbank. A few sent in cartoons, among them H.M. Bateman, whose *Growth of Woman* provided a (not unambiguously positive) view on female emancipation (see page 33), while George E. Studdy submitted an early depiction of his cartoon character Bonzo the Dog, who would go on to become an international celebrity. Some subjects were very personal indeed: Albert Goodwin offered, in the manner of a confession, a watercolour of *An Egg from the Only Nest I Robbed*.

Other contributors expressed in their letters to Princess Marie Louise their aim to demonstrate the best of their personal skill, either in technique or subject.

Far right: Rose Barton
(1856–1929)

A Child by a Paling Fence,
1922, pencil, pen and ink
and watercolour

RCIN 926806

Right: Florence Callcott
(active 1866–1938)

Head of a Girl in Profile,
c.1922, pencil and
bodycolour

RCIN 926882

Mrs.F.J.Callcott,
[Florence Newman,R.M.S]

Rose Barton, R.W.S.

George Cockram noted his wish to 'make the water colour as representative of my work as is possible on so small a scale', while S. Arthur Lindsey wrote that, as a miniature painter, 'I venture to suggest that my Contribution be a miniature miniature'. William Luker explained that, 'Having made a special study of animal portraiture I would like to be so represented', while John de Walton offered 'a dashing military subject, which is typical of my work'. For the sculptor Florence Callcott, it was a challenge to represent her three-dimensional practice on flat paper. She eventually produced a monochrome painting intended to resemble a relief sculpture, but apologised for the delay in submission, explaining that the solution to her dilemma 'took some thinking out'.

A significant group of prints and drawings present the varied reaction of the country's artists to the shock of the First World War. Among those included were works by the brothers Paul Nash and John Northcote Nash, both of whom had served as soldiers and had created arresting paintings of the conflict. Paul Nash's *Dymchurch Wall* is the depiction of a motif which the artist repeatedly studied during his recovery from a post-traumatic breakdown in 1921. Paul Nash's contemporary at the Slade School of Art, Christopher Richard Wynne Nevinson (like Nash an official war artist), submitted a pen and ink drawing of the sun over an idealised continental roofscape (see page 49). Another soldier-artist, Alexander Proudfoot, contributed a pencil and watercolour drawing, which represents an early concept for the war memorial he was to produce for Bearsden Cross in East Dunbartonshire, unveiled in 1924. Eric Kennington, who had specialised in depicting soldiers in the trenches, agreed to provide a work but seems never to have delivered it. Of all those with direct experience, the ambulance driver Robert Spence provided the most immediate depiction of the war in an etching of a casualty being attended to in the trenches.

While some had experienced the conflict first hand, others took its aftermath as their subject: the Edinburgh artist Emily Murray Paterson submitted a watercolour of Ypres made in the summer of 1919, showing a scarred landscape of trees stripped bare by gunfire, while Alexander Warren Dow depicted a road in Picardy, the scene of fierce battles along the Somme. Emily Mary Bibbens Warren sent a watercolour entitled *The Empire's Shrine*, showing the tomb of the Unknown Warrior at Westminster Abbey, and John Charles Dollman provided an atmospheric scene of the Cenotaph in London on Armistice Day (see page 86). Perhaps too,

John Northcote Nash (1893–1977)

'Winter scene' (Whiteleaf, Princes Risborough), 1922, watercolour, bodycolour and pencil

RCIN 927216

Paul Nash (1889–1946)

Dymchurch Wall, 1922, pen and ink and watercolour

RCIN 927217

Emily Murray Paterson (1855–1934)

Ypres, Summer 1919, *c*.1922, pencil, watercolour and bodycolour

RCIN 927255

E.M.Paterson, R.S.W.

some of the depictions of traditional, rural, lifestyles were provided in the same spirit of reflection as Thomas Hardy's poem 'In Time of "The Breaking of Nations"', published during the First World War and included among Hardy's contribution to the books in the Dolls' House Library. As Hardy writes of 'a man harrowing clods, in a slow silent walk', whose activity is unaffected by the disruption of war, so Cecil Ross Burnett's *Women Gleaning*

"Robert Spencer".

Alexander Proudfoot, ARSA.

Robert Spence (1871–1964)

A Casualty in the Trenches, *c*.1922, etching and drypoint

RCIN 927388

Spence's name was misspelled on the mount

Alexander Proudfoot (1878–1957)

1914–1918, *c*.1922, pencil and watercolour

RCIN 927288

C. Ross Burnett, R.I.

Herbert Cole.

Cecil Ross Burnett (1872–1933)

Women Gleaning, c.1922, pencil
and watercolour

RCIN 926870

Herbert Cole (1867–1930)

Ex-Soldiers' Homes in Chadwick Road,
1922, pen and ink and watercolour

RCIN 926901

and the elderly man and young boy shown in W.B. Fortescue's *Putting in Broccoli* must continue their work as the year turns, regardless of conflict.

For two artists, the invitation to contribute provided a means to protest against the poverty and distress of the early 1920s. Herbert Cole submitted a scene with the title *Ex-Soldiers' Homes in Chadwick Road*. His accompanying letter sought to bring to royal attention 'the homes in which Ex-Soldiers of Camberwell and their families have been living for the past several months. These miserable shelters are made of tarpaulin sheets patched with pieces of old linoleum, and have been erected

outside a disused brewery from which these families have been evicted.' The Irish artist J.B.S. MacIlwaine also used the opportunity of his invitation to voice his concern for the welfare of others, declining to take part unless he received 5 guineas to help those who were left homeless and desolate by the Irish Civil War. His request was denied (see page 83).

From social protests to society portraits, the fascination of the Dolls' House portfolios is their presentation of a moment in British art. They bring together artists of different generations, from those who had established their artistic approach many years previously, to those who were still exploring the potential of their skill. To place the watercolour by Thomas Hunt alongside those of brothers Paul and John Nash, for example, is to see the breadth of the British landscape tradition, how these artists born nearly forty years apart addressed the challenges and potential of the countryside around them in works which speak the same language, but with very varying accents.

When C.E. Hughes wrote about the prints and drawings in the Library in *The Book of the Queen's Dolls' House*, published in 1924, he approached the collection as a charming fancy, imagining that 'small dolls … will surely love, no less than their elders, some at least of the contents of the cabinets, for there is an almost infinite variety'. At a distance of 100 years, the collection of works on paper formed by Princess Marie Louise and her advisers looks less like whimsy and more like a significant attempt to capture the artistic pulse of a nation. Even though some of those invited were unable or unwilling to participate, the range of work represented remains impressive. As an assemblage of over 700 works created at a single moment, by artists of all ages selected as the most significant of their time, the scope and ambition of the Dolls' House prints and drawings are unparalleled: there is no comparable collection of works on paper in existence. Each contributing artist may have added, in Fullwood's words, an 'atom' to the whole, but those atoms came together to form a collection of tremendous significance for our understanding of British art, and artists, in the early years of the 1920s.

Thos. Hunt, R.S.W.

Thomas Hunt
(1854–1929)

Evening, Loch Lomond, 1922, watercolour and bodycolour

RCIN 927096

'IT WILL HAVE IN THE FUTURE SUCH INESTIMABLE VALUE'

· · · · · · · · · ·

AT THE END OF HER MINIATURE manuscript *A Note of Explanation*, Vita Sackville-West wonders if anyone will care to ruin their eyesight by reading the books in the Dolls' House Library. They are worth the eyestrain. While printed copies of the contributed manuscripts convey the charm and ingenuity of the contents of the little books, they cannot communicate the thrill of seeing the bright, intricate bindings filled with the specially commissioned, handwritten words of writers who enthusiastically entered into the joy of the project.

And it is not only the manuscripts which should be celebrated. The Library of Queen Mary's Dolls' House is a miniature monument to culture in the 1920s. The artworks record the wealth of artistic ability in the nation, while the bookbindings are an outstanding example of what the finest binders of the time could achieve. The music, specially chosen for the occasion, represents what was being played and appreciated, and the autograph books record many of the most significant figures in public life. The important collection of printed books, including many miniaturised specially, make the Library complete.

This first full study of the contents of Queen Mary's Dolls' House Library is an overview of this significant collection and there is a great deal more to be investigated. Deeper exploration of the intentions of the contributors, and of the themes found amongst their works, will illuminate, amongst much else, studies of folklore and the First World War. The contributions and correspondence of the artists and writers involved will provide greater understanding not only of their work but also of the artistic and literary networks in which they operated, and will prove invaluable to students of early twentieth-century art, literature and cultural life; likewise, a study of those who refused to contribute or who were omitted will be instructive. The bookbindings, capturing the essence of one of the greatest eras in binding history, also merit further research from historians of the book and of the Arts and Crafts movement.

E.V. Lucas wrote of the Dolls' House as being a memorial of one, unending day that would 'have in the future such inestimable value to social historians'. He was right: the miniature library he collected with Princess

Marie Louise is a fascinating window into the past. It gives us an opportunity to better understand those who contributed, by seeing what they felt was worth recording for posterity. In the miniature books and artworks we can read the contributors' and organisers' need both to escape from war and modernity, and to remember and celebrate them. We can share in the delight they took in creating something both historic and whimsical, and fully appreciate how a very small book can be a very great treasure.

'The End'
Fougasse (1887–1965)
J. Smith, 1922
RCIN 1171321

157

SELECT BIBLIOGRAPHY

Further details for each of the Dolls' House Library books can be found at **www.rct.uk/collection**.

The primary archive for correspondence relating to the Dolls' House Library is at the Royal Archives, Windsor Castle, RA VIC/ADD/A/18/ML.

Benson, A.C., and Sir Lawrence Weaver, eds, *The Book of the Queen's Dolls' House* (London, 1924)

Bondy, Louis W., *Miniature Books: Their History from their Beginnings to the Present Day* (London, 1981)

Bown, Nicola, *Fairies in Nineteenth-Century Art and Literature* (Cambridge, 2001)

Broomhead, Frank, *The Zaehnsdorfs (1842–1947): Craft Bookbinders* (Pinner, 1986)

Burnett, Archie, *The Letters of A.E. Housman*, vol. 1 (Oxford, 2007)

Farr, Diana, *Gilbert Cannan: A Georgian Prodigy* (London, 1978)

Lambton, Lucinda, *The Queen's Dolls' House* (London, 2017)

Lucas, Audrey, *E.V. Lucas: A Portrait* (London, 1939)

Lucas, E.V., ed., *The Book of the Queen's Dolls' House Library* (London, 1924)

Milne, A.A., *It's Too Late Now: The Autobiography of a Writer* (London, 1939)

Oxford Dictionary of National Biography

Percy, Clayre and Jane Ridley, eds, *The Letters of Edwin Lutyens to his wife, Lady Emily* (London, 1985)

Pope-Hennessy, James, *Queen Mary* (London, 2019)

Princess Marie Louise, *My Memories of Six Reigns* (London, 1956)

Ridley, Jane, *Edwin Lutyens: His Life, his Wife, his Work* (London, 2003)

Sassoon, Siegfried, ed. Rupert Hart-Davis, *Diaries, 1920–22* (London and Boston, 1981)

Shepherd, Rob, *The Cinderella of the Arts: A Short History of Sangorski & Sutcliffe* (London, 2015)

Telfer, Kevin, *Peter Pan's First XI: The Extraordinary Story of J.M. Barrie's Cricket Team* (London, 2010)

Toole-Stott, Raymond, *A Bibliography of the Works of W. Somerset Maugham* (London, 1973)

ACKNOWLEDGEMENTS

Four chapters in this book are the work of contributors:

The Room
Kathryn Jones

'The Little Books Look Divine'
Sophie Kelly

'One of Royalty's Favourite Occupations'
Emma Stuart

'I Shall be Pleased to Add my Atom of Art'
Kate Heard

Thank you to all my colleagues and friends who have assisted with this book: to Sophie Kelly and Elizabeth Silverton, whose dedication to this project has been invaluable; to my colleagues in the Royal Library, Andrew Brown, Emily Hannam, Stella Panayotova, Rachel Scott, Emma Stuart and Bridget Wright, for all their support and advice; to Glenn Bartley and Irene Campden in the Royal Bindery for guidance and for caring for the miniature books, and to Matt Stockl who demonstrated how a miniature book is bound and decorated; to colleagues in the Print Room and Royal Archives, for their help; to knowledgeable Dolls' House colleagues Beth Jones and Kathryn Jones; to all in the Royal Collection's Publishing and Picture Library teams, especially Anjali Bulley, Karen Lawson and Kate Owen; to the photographers Richard Shellabear and Eva Zielinska-Millar for expert photography of delicate items; to Lucinda Kelly and Belinda Kim for all their help; to Michèle Barrett for her insights; to Elizabeth Hawkesworth for information on the *Birthday Book*; to Martin Lutyens of the Lutyens Trust for his help; to Sarah Waters for her Virginia Woolf reference; to Sarah Kane for her skilled editing; and to erstwhile writing partner Oliver Urquhart Irvine, instrumental in the planning of this book. Finally, thank you to Robin, Harry and Isobel, for their understanding.

Published 2024 by Royal Collection Trust
York House, St James's Palace
London SW1A 1BQ

Royal Collection Trust / © His Majesty King Charles III 2024

All images are Royal Collection Trust / © His Majesty
King Charles III 2024 unless otherwise indicated below.

Pages 12, 29, 36, 77, 109: © National Portrait Gallery, London;
Page 13: © Hulton Archive/Getty Images; Page 20: © Candia
Lutyens, Lutyens Trust Photo Archive; Page 21: © Royal
Institute of British Architects, London; Page 32: © 2024 Image
copyright The Metropolitan Museum of Art/Art Resource/
Scala, Florence; Page 33: © H.M. Bateman Designs/www.
hmbateman.com; Pages 37, 38, 71: All rights reserved; Pages 38,
40, 49, 50, 56, 83: The Royal Archives. All rights reserved;
Page 43: © Reproduced with permission of Curtis Brown Group
Ltd on behalf of the Beneficiaries of the Estate of Vita Sackville-
West; Page 44: © National Trust/Anthony Lambert. All rights
reserved; Page 69: Private Collection; Photo © Christie's
Images/Bridgeman Images; Page 70: Estate of Herbert
James Gunn; Page 76: Toronto Star Photograph Archive,
Courtesy of Toronto Public Library; Page 103: © Mary Evans
Picture Library/Peter & Dawn Cope Collection; Page 105:
© NMPFT/Glenn Hill/Science & Society Picture Library.
All rights reserved; Page 109: Reproduced with the permission
of Curtis Brown, London, on behalf of Churchill Heritage
Ltd © Churchill Heritage Ltd; Page 113: With thanks to
the Sangorski & Sutcliffe Archive; Page 114: With thanks to
Matthew Stockl and Andreas Maroulis; Page 135: © Illustrated
London News Ltd/Mary Evans Picture Library; Page 137:
Margaret Morris Movement International Ltd; Page 148:
Courtesy of The Munnings Art Museum

With grateful thanks to the Dolls' House binderies: Birdsall,
Hatchards, Riviere, Sangorski & Sutcliffe and Zaehnsdorf

Every effort has been made to trace and credit all
known copyright or reproduction rights holders; the
publishers apologise for any errors or omissions and
welcome these being brought to their attention.

All rights reserved. Except as permitted under current
legislation, no part of this work may be photocopied,
stored in a retrieval system, published, performed in
public, adapted, broadcast, transmitted, recorded or
reproduced in any form or by any means, without
the prior permission of the copyright owner.

ISBN 978 1 909741 57 7
103863

10 9 8 7 6 5 4 3 2 1

A catalogue record of this book is available from
the British Library

Publisher: Kate Owen
Designer: Matthew Wilson
Project Managers: Elizabeth Silverton & Anjali Bulley
Production Manager: Sarah Tucker
Editors: Sarah Kane & Bev Zimmern
Colour reproduction: DL Imaging
Printed on Claro silk 150gsm
Printed and bound in Wales by Gomer Press